WAS THERE THEN **oasis** A PHOTOGRAPHIC JOURNEY BY ╲

with text by Daniela Soave

ABOUT THE AUTHORS

JILL FURMANOVSKY spent her childhood in Rhodesia (now Zimbabwe), born of German and Lithuanian parents. Her father, an architect by profession, had a passion for music and photography, and in 1965, when the family left Africa for England due to the worsening political situation, the young Jill was devastated that her father was forced to leave behind his darkroom and the largest private collection of jazz records in Bulawayo. Growing up in London in the sixties, Jill found comfort in the pop scene, *Ready Steady Go* and The Beatles. Aware that art schools had nurtured musicians and many of her heroes she enrolled for a textile course at the Central School of Art and Design in 1972. The syllabus included a two-week crash course in photography that was the only formal instruction in the art that she then fell in love with. During those same two weeks she went to see Yes at the Rainbow, pushing her luck and taking photos among the accredited photographers. A fortnight later she was the venue's offical in-house photographer. Throughout her career Jill has taken photos of everyone in music, from The Clash to Bob Marley, Pink Floyd to The Police, from The Sex Pistols to Oasis.

DANIELA SOAVE spent her first years playing tennis racket to The Beatles and has been writing about music for twenty years. She first worked with Jill Furmanovsky shortly after moving to London from Scotland at the end of the seventies. Over the years, Daniela has been a deputy editor at *Scotland on Sunday*, a commissioning editor at the *Sunday Telegraph* and the *Radio Times* and founding deputy editor at *Sky Magazine*. She has also broadcast for radio and television and has contributed to *Elle*, *GQ*, the *Observer* and the *Independent*, the *Daily Telegraph* and the *Daily Mail*. She loves music, art, and post-gig parties that are still going strong at 10 a.m.

ACKNOWLEDGEMENTS:
Braco Ado Sigal
Merle Moustafa
Daniela Soave
Yvonne McConaghy
David Bennet
Sam Frenkel
Nick Segal
Vicki McIvor at Breakthrough Management
Hazel Westcott
Neil Scott & co.
Neville Brody & Research Studios
Chris Levine & I.C.
Mark George
Marcus Russell, Alec Mckinlay & Kat Rumens, Katherine Richmond, Christine Biller at Ignition
Johnny Hopkins, Alan McGee, Emma Greengrass, Vanessa Cotton, Karen McIlmurray & Tones Sansome at Creation Records
Brian Cannon & all at Microdot
Maggie Mouzakitis (tour manager)
Jason Rhodes (Oasis crew)
Roger Nowell (Oasis crew)
David Massey (Sony USA)
Linda Gibson (Sony UK)
Stephen Digby & Damon Parker at Withers Solicitors
Jake Lingwood
Dan Newman

LOVE & GRATITUDE TO:
Jack & Eva Furmanovsky
Ron Berglas, Leah Berglas xxx
Michele Easterman
Yvonne Gordon
Dr Ruth Davis & Frenchie
Dr Marion Reiff
Jane Ripley
Joy Sapeika
Helga Sigvaldadottir

EXHIBITION TEAM:
Shelley Warren at Exhibit-A
Saul Radomsky
Steven Mecleod, Craig Taylor & Mark Foxwell at Primary Colour
Ian Cartwright & Harry Matthews at Quicksilver
Joe's Basement
Ceta Colour
Mark Tinkler at Imation
Fiona O'Brien
Maria Florey at Epson
Conal & Scott at MCP
Tapestry

First published in Great Britain in 1997

1 3 5 7 9 10 8 6 4 2

Photographs © Jill Furmanovsky 1997
Text © Daniela Soave 1997 (except for captions, which are individually attributed)

Ebury Press
Random House, 20 Vauxhall Bridge Road, London SW1V 2SA

Random House Australia Pty Limited
20 Alfred Street, Milsons Point, Sydney, New South Wales 2061, Australia

Random House New Zealand Limited
18 Poland Road, Glenfield, Auckland 10, New Zealand

Random House South Africa (Pty) Limited
Endulini, 5A Jubilee Road, Parktown 2193, South Africa

Random House UK Limited Reg. No. 954009

A CIP catalogue record for this book is available from the British Library

ISBN 0 09 186318 X

Cover design: Research Studio   Book design: Dan Newman

Printed and bound in Portugal by Printer Portuguesa L.d.a.
Papers used by Ebury Press are natural, recyclable products made from wood grown in sustainable forests.

THIS BOOK IS DEDICATED TO OASIS'S
BIGGEST FANS: NOEL, LIAM, BONEHEAD,
GUIGS AND WHITEY. WITH DEEP LOVE
AND AFFECTION FROM JILL.

INTRODUCTION

Like everything to do with Oasis, this photographic project escalated from modest aspirations and spiralled into the stratosphere. 'It's not over until it's over,' said Noel when the band began work on their third album in autumn 1996, much to the relief of a few million Oasis fans, myself included. I thought: I've got loads of good photographs of the band taken over the last three years, why not put on an exhibition of my Oasis pictures, when the next album comes out?

I mentioned the idea to Noel while they were in Abbey Road at the very beginning of the recording process. He liked it, so I asked, 'Have you got a title for me?' thinking he could mull it over in the months to come. Without pausing at all, Noel said, 'Well this album is going to be called *Be Here Now*, so it's obvious innit, yours has got to be called *Was There Then'.* A year later as the project takes off, it seems it was always part of the masterplan . . .

Coinciding with a technical revolution in photography, which includes the whole spectrum of digital manipulation and inkjet printing, the *Was There Then* exhibition hopes to break all boundaries in terms of defining what a 'photographic exhibition' is. For starters, 80 per cent of this accompanying book, which in many ways is a catalogue for the exhibition, was 'printed' in a computer rather than a darkroom – a technical first for me.

The text has been written by Daniela Soave. As well as having the best antennae in the music business – it was she who introduced me to Oasis, amongst others – she is one of the finest writers on rock this country has produced. Having accompanied the band on more than one tour and drunk them under the table, she is amply equipped to reflect on their power and glory as well as their fractures.

Finally, I am writing this introduction from a hotel room in San Francisco. Last night I went to see 'The best there was and best there'll ever be' play on the same bill as the mighty U2 in a stadium in Oakland. It was a night of music so blissful and inspiring no one wanted to leave. The last sight I had, before catching a ride home with Bonehead and keyboard player Mike in the early hours of this morning, was of Noel and The Edge roaring with laughter in a corner, while Liam, in full throttle, sang and air-guitared the whole of the new Oasis album in Bono's ear, eventually inspiring the latter to put his arm around him and join in on the choruses.

I'm going to see them both again tonight – might take a few pictures. Yeah, still mad for it!

Jill Furmanovsky

San Francisco 19 June 1997

BE HERE NOW

THE MAGICAL MYSTERY TOUR

THIRTY YEARS ON

May 2, 1997. A new government begins its first day in power following a landslide victory: the sun is blazing and the mood of the nation is euphoric. Not as exuberant perhaps as the man who walks into a London photographic studio bearing the fruits of the past nine months' work, for he is Noel Gallagher and in his hand he's clutching the test pressing of the new Oasis album, *Be Here Now*.

Last night he was invited to join Tony Blair at the Labour Party's celebratory bash at the Royal Festival Hall. The feeling of change is all-encompassing. Thirty years ago the summer of love washed over Great Britain: music, fashion and art formed the backbone of the new optimism. Everything in the garden was groovy and the nation's youth were head gardeners. Now, for the first time in three decades, that sensibility prevails once more. London is, according to international style bibles, *where it's at* and the new government seems keen to align itself with all that is cool in British youth culture.

Instead of joining the revellers, Gallagher chose to return to the studio to supervise the mastering of his album. There was never any question about which option he would take. In three short years, Noel Gallagher might have been transformed from a mouthy, Northern nobody into a prime member of the rock elite, courted by fashion designers, media moguls and politicians alike, but he never forgets what put him there: his all-consuming passion, music. His own.

He heads straight for the photographic studio's stereo, inserts the CD and cranks up the volume. A burst of guitar blasts through the speakers and a satisfied grin spreads over his face. Like a Mexican wave, the smile ricochets over the faces of the other members of the band – Liam Gallagher, bassist Paul 'Guigs' McGuigan, drummer Alan White and guitarist Paul 'Bonehead' Arthurs – as Liam's vocals snarl into life. Liam punches the air with a salutary gesture while his brother, only half-jokingly, starts to play air guitar.

One of the remarkable things about Oasis is that they remain the band's greatest fans. If they weren't part of it, they'd go out and buy the records. As they wait for the photo session to begin, they bask in the spring sunshine of the studio yard, nodding and laughing at one

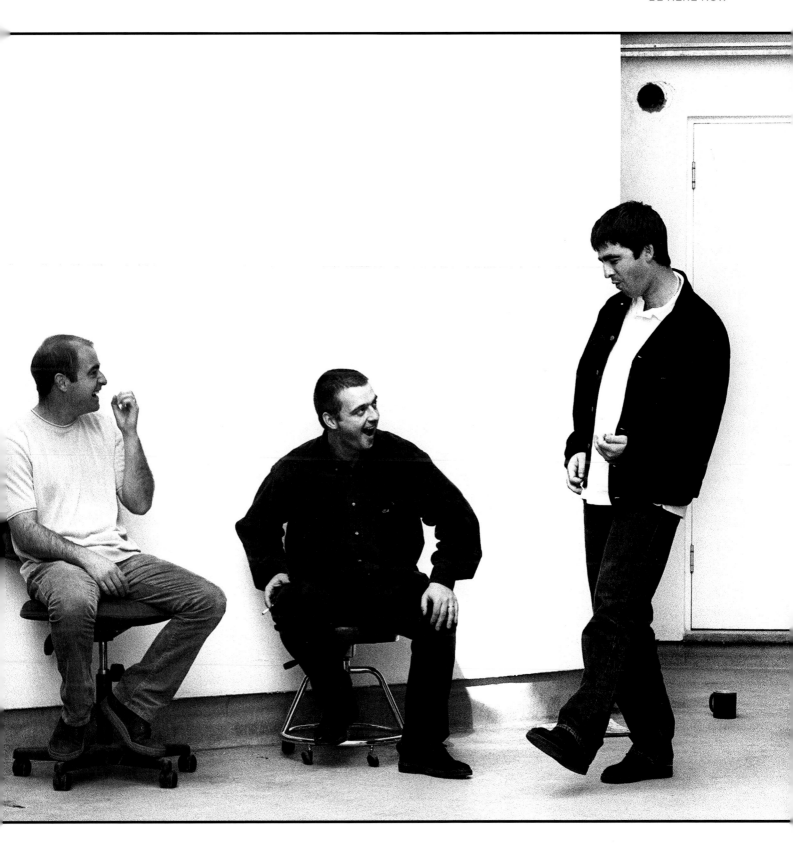

another, but mostly looking in admiration at the man they affectionately call The Boss. *Be Here Now* is their most ambitious, finely crafted record to date and this is the first time that all five have been in each other's company to hear it in its entirety.

Since their ninth, ill-fated American tour came to an abrupt halt in September 1996, amidst an unprecedented tabloid frenzy which even ignited the more sedate broadsheet press, the five men have spent little time together. During the nine months spent making the new album, there were few occasions when all of them were in the studio at the same time. Today, therefore, is as much about rekindling band unity as it is about having their photographs taken.

Looking at their relaxed faces, the prolonged hiatus seems to have done Oasis the power of good. Since January 1994, when they began their well-planned assault on the world, their lives have been dominated by a rigorous diet of touring, recording and promotion. If they weren't on the road they could be found in the studio. If they weren't in the studio they'd be making videos. And if they weren't doing that there was always an endless line of print journalists and television crews waiting to use up what little time there was left.

With a gruelling schedule that meant an endless string of tours in Britain, Europe and America, more often than not back-to-back, the band were never in one place long enough to let the dust settle, which might be fine for demonstrating a seriously un-rock'n'roll work ethic or gaining a well-deserved reputation as one of the most awesome live acts of the decade, but useless for preventing their heads from getting mashed. In the world of rock'n'roll, success almost depends on making a pact with the devil: no one escapes unscathed.

With fame and fortune came the inevitability of coming to terms with living in a goldfish bowl. I remember walking down a London street with Bonehead in May 1995, at the time of their first number one, 'Some Might Say', when Oasis were first becoming public property. It was an experience that he couldn't yet accept. 'Do you know who I am?' he would demand of a perfect stranger, who would look back at him as if he were mad, before replying, 'You're Bonehead'. After this happened three times in a row, Bonehead looked seriously depressed. For Noel and Liam, this high-profile pressure has been multiplied a hundredfold.

Prior to the US bust-up, there had been signs that life in the fast lane was becoming too much to bear, most notably when Oasis cancelled Japanese and Australian tours at the beginning of 1995 and later the same year when Guigs succumbed to nervous exhaustion. Because so much was at stake, the old sticking-plaster solution was applied: a short healing time and then back to work. It's easy with hindsight to see that it would have been better to have addressed the problem earlier by scheduling some time off, but when your star is in the ascendant, time waits for no one.

This enforced break, caused by taking their time with the new album, has given them the much-needed breathing space to enjoy for the first time the results of their years of hard work. Each has bought a new home that, just a few years earlier, they could only have dreamed of. Each has been able to fly off to some tropical idyll with their loved ones to escape prying eyes. And, most important of all, they've been able to get off the crazed media merry-go-round and reclaim normality, something that has been denied them for too long.

Back in the photographic studio, it's obvious that the band is raring to go. The air is peppered with typical Oasis expressions – 'Fucking tops!' and 'Mad for it!' – as the CD is played over and over again. Although *Be Here Now* won't be released for some months, this playback heralds the start of a new era for a band which, less than a year earlier, had been written off by the media. Over the next few weeks, as plans for the album, singles, interviews and gigs are put into place, the enormous Oasis machine will crank into gear. And, judging from the buoyant mood this morning, not a moment too soon. While the band indulge in some light-hearted back-slapping, in the studio indoors Jill Furmanovsky is preparing for the shoot. A small, dark-haired woman who has photographed everyone in the rock aristocracy worth photographing over the past twenty-five years, she is the unofficial – yet acknowledged – principal Oasis photographer.

I first met Furmanovsky eighteen years ago when I worked for the music press. In those days there were few female journalists and fewer female photographers, so we became a team. Watching her in action is mesmerising. Because she is unobtrusive, half the time her subjects don't realise who she is. She is less interested in conventional publicity shots, where the subjects stand awkwardly, grim-faced, in a row, than in photographs that get to the soul, or those that place a moment in time. She uses the minimum of equipment. And by cutting away the crap, she gets results that her contemporaries can only aspire to. I would call her an organic photographer.

In 1994 I spent a week with Oasis in Japan, reporting on their first tour in the Far East. I think they were somewhat thrown by my arrival, even though I had interviewed Noel previously. For a start, I was a good ten years older than most of them. I was a mother. And I was writing for a nancy-boy's magazine, *GQ*. It seemed to me that the only way I would get to the true core of Oasis was to take them on at their own game, so for the next seven days I did my best to drink them under the table and stay up later than any of them. It worked. At the end of the week, Noel Gallagher proclaimed that not only was I 'fucking mad', but a bad influence on his band.

During my trip, I was accompanied by Oasis spokesman Johnny Hopkins and a photographer who normally specialises in fashion, Will Camden. If Furmanovsky is an unconventional photographer, Hopkins is equally untypical of the average press officer. I nicknamed him the dormouse in the teapot because he seems to exist on another planet. Those who are fooled by his vague manner fail to realise that his vision of how the band should be presented is inspired, or that his dedication to them is unswerving. As for Camden, this was his first foray (and, I believe, his last!) into the world of rock reporting. The pictures he produced were vibrant and enthralling, yet every day there was tension between him and Liam, which usually ended in Liam storming off on his own, his wild mutterings peppered with expletives. Liam, it was evident, didn't respond well to being told what to do, even if it were simply to stand next to Noel and tilt his chin. By contrast, I noticed that although he would still mutter under his breath whenever Margaret Mouzakitis, their formidable Greek-American tour manager, issued orders, he would comply. Could it be that he responded better to women?

A conversation with Hopkins confirmed this, so I told him that there was somebody he – and Oasis – should meet. When, months later, Jill photographed their gig at the Cambridge Corn Exchange, her atmospheric, beautifully-crafted pictures confirmed to them that they need look no further. She has been on board ever since.

During the three years that she has been associated with Oasis, Jill has photographed them on the road, at video shoots, in performance and backstage. Her reportage style suits the band, who are uneasy about being photographed formally. As Johnny Hopkins says, 'They're real-life characters and the photographs reflect that. We don't want anything posed because it's not Oasis. Some people like posing: they don't. When you've got a band whose faces are known all over the place, you want to see their personalities, their vibe. Jill witnesses things that are a bit off the wall, that you're not normally going to see. She's in places that no one else is going to be.'

Because new images will be required to satisfy press demand once media interest is rekindled with the imminent release of the new album, Furmanovsky has today booked the band for a two-day session. The previous day, as voters went to the polls, the band were instructed to turn up at her north London studio to take part in a magical mystery tour.

Accustomed to receiving meticulous, finely detailed tour itineraries, the concept intrigued them. They turned up at the appointed hour to discover a plush, silver but – compared to what Oasis have become accustomed to – diminutive Winnebago that was poised to take them to a secret destination.

Once on board, the bus takes them to Richmond to have their holograms taken for the forthcoming *Was There Then* exhibition. The process is quite mind-boggling: lasers silently scan the face and bounce off mirrors to create an eerie, three-dimensional likeness. Conveniently, the studio was next to a pub where Jill had arranged a running tab – music to their ears! Once that session was completed, she added, they would be moving on to the faded elegance of a disused stately home which would form an unusual backdrop. The day was a resounding success.

Furmanovsky knows only too well that, perhaps more than other bands, Oasis have a low boredom threshold, and in order to guarantee their cooperation she has to keep things moving. The first day's shoot, with its two very different locations, has worked well and she hopes to repeat her success today by trying a more formal studio shot than both she and the band are used to, before rewarding them with yet another surprise location.

The lighting ready and the backdrop in place, she calls them into the studio. As the band troop in from the yard, Noel turns to me and quietly asks, 'So what do you think?' This is typical of him. He has supreme confidence in his work, some would say bordering on arrogance, but always he will canvass opinions , whether it's about a gig, an interview, a song or in this case, the new album. Even more interestingly, once I have given him the answer he wants – not a difficult task given the quality of the material – he turns without a word and walks away.

Once in the studio, Oasis huddle self consciously in front of the lens. Without so much as a word, Liam sizes up the situation and takes control. He starts to lark about, ducking and diving between the others, whooping, laughing and yelling. Instantly the mood is caught by Bonehead, Alan, Guigs and Noel. Incredibly, they start Morris dancing to their own record – surely the most absurd sight one could expect to see of them.

Liam's antics are becoming a regular part of an Oasis session. For group shots at least, while the others are content to stand in a fixed position and stare into the lens, he has grown impatient with the all-too-familiar pose and now tries to inject movement and humour into the proceedings – something that his older brother doesn't seem to appreciate. But Furmanovsky has observed a sea-change in Liam: 'He's becoming increasingly interested in the visual side, and is willing to make a contribution.'

'It's boring, isn't it?' says Liam of the standard pose. 'It's boring to look at and it's boring to stand there.'

Within half an hour the shot is in the bag. Fuelled by lager and adrenalin, the band are eagerly awaiting lunch, having been promised an Indian takeaway. As they hover round the kitchen, Bonehead picks up a pile of Furmanovsky's photographs and starts leafing through them, laughing to himself. He stops at one of him and Guigs, standing outside a vast American tour bus.

'What sticks in your memory most about those American tours?' I ask him. He looks at me as if I have taken leave of my senses. 'I don't know,' he replies. 'It's all a blur. You know what it's like: you've been on the road with us. Make it up.'

Later, Jill will ask him a similar question about their Maine Road gig: what do you remember about it? Fuck all, really, comes the reply.

The moment is pierced by the return of the studio assistant, who is carrying several buckets of Kentucky Fried Chicken. As she starts to explain apologetically what happened to the Indian takeaway, her voice is drowned out by enthusiastic whoops of pleasure from the band, who descend upon the feast with the ferocity of a shoal of piranha fish. It seems only seconds before they leave the table littered with debris.

It's time to get on the bus. Jill announces our next destination: a King's Cross snooker hall she has booked for the afternoon. As the bus sets off in busy Friday-afternoon traffic, she explains the reasons behind her choices of locations of the past two days.

'I think one of the reasons we work well together is I don't actually work for Oasis. Or for the record company, for that matter. I don't usually organise anything. I go in and take the pictures, record what's going on. But on this occasion *I* was the reason for getting the band together, so *I* had to decide what to do with them, and I wanted to choose places where I knew they would be comfortable. That's really the essence of everything we've done over the last two days."

As the bus noses its way out of traffic, I'm reminded of the early days. Oasis now travel on mega-coaches complete with a large entourage, but today it's just them, us and one bodyguard. Liam, particularly, is enjoying himself as he stares out of the window, daring anyone to catch his eye. When drivers or pedestrians make eye contact, it's followed by a swift double-take on their part, especially when Liam proffers his trademark V-fingered salute.

As his interest wanes in what's going on outside the bus, he turns his attention to his fellow travellers. Soon they are comparing their latest toys and acquisitions: Rolex watches, mobile phones, ludicrously expensive designer lighters that you just know are going to get lost within forty-eight hours. Bonehead reveals that his two-year-old daughter has names for his Rolls Royce and his recently-acquired Aston Martin ('Shopping Car' and 'Daddy's Silly Car'), while Liam gets the others up to speed on his latest home-improvement plans. Noel is the subject of much teasing thanks to having finally succumbed to the temptation of a mobile phone after years of insisting he would never, ever, possess one.

As I listen to their conversation, a thought crosses my mind: can this be the same bunch of people who were once lauded as drug-taking, alcohol-swilling, hotel-trashing shag-monsters?

Before I can put this to the band, the bus draws up directly outside the snooker hall and we are quickly ushered through a side door. The room is vast and has two unexpected bonuses – a bar and a jukebox. As quick as a flash, Noel is standing over the latter, scanning the menu and shoving money into the slot as he discovers a rich seam of Beatles, Hendrix and Stones. 'Can you turn up the volume?' he calls over to the woman behind the bar, where Liam is already getting the beers in.

As Bonehead, Alan, Guigs and Liam start to rack up a frame, Noel retreats to a corner, where he submerges himself in the music and observes the proceedings. Although he's obviously enjoying himself, it is also apparent that, whether deliberately or not, he's holding back. Noel has always said that he's a natural loner, but I've another theory. He'll probably say it's bollocks, but as the acknowledged boss of the outfit, there's a bit of manager/workforce psychology going on there. Just as conventional heads of department believe it's unwise to fraternise too much with their staff, so Noel Gallagher prefers to take his entertainment elsewhere.

Liam, meanwhile, has interrupted his game to claim another beer and talk to the lad behind the bar. Although he has a reputation for being sullen and unapproachable, Gallagher Junior is in fact more accessible than his brother. He is genuinely happy, as long as he makes the first move, to speak to anybody and seems truly interested in what they have to say. The boy behind the bar is momentarily stunned, but soon the pair are deep in conversation.

Sensing that the action is taking place at the opposite end of the room, Noel gets up and quickly walks towards Jill, who is photographing Bonehead. He whispers something in her ear and motions for her to follow him back down the hall. He picks up a piece of chalk and starts to scrawl some words across the darts blackboard, pausing momentarily for Jill to capture each word.

Be.

Here.

Now.

Satisfied with his handiwork, he sits down underneath it and motions for her to take a snap.

Back at the bar, his eyes on the action, Liam turns to me and says: 'If I want to say something, will you write it for me?' It is a touching moment. I have a lot of time for Liam. It would never occur to him to do anything else but tell the truth, which is why one can understand his mood swings and tantrums. Remember him telling reporters why he couldn't fly off with the rest of the band to start the last American tour: he had to stay behind to help Patsy find another home. Other people might have diplomatically – but dishonestly – pleaded a five-day virus.

Perhaps years of being told at school that he would never amount to anything has dulled his confidence in the written word. But Liam is as sharp as a pin and, as inspiration strikes, he's off, grabbing the chalk and scribbling furiously without any assistance. That task out of the way, all five sit down at the table and get stuck in to another beer.

Suddenly, the door beside them bursts open and a helmeted motorbike messenger, delivering more film, strides into the room, oblivious to the drinkers on his right. Liam yells at him and the messenger turns to face them, stepping back in noticeable amazement when it dawns on him who he is seeing. Hastily putting his bottle on the table, Liam jumps up and starts to waltz across the room with the startled messenger, who's so surprised that he starts to dance as if it were the most natural thing in the world to be waltzing to Jimi Hendrix with Liam Gallagher as your partner.

Noel is getting restless. He's keen for a change. He vetoes the suggestion of an old-fashioned barber's shop and suggests driving down to Whitehall and storming 10 Downing Street. Afternoon tea with Tony, perhaps? An interesting proposition, but the rush-hour traffic will be against us. Instead, Jill suggests walking out into nearby King's Cross and seeing what happens there. While Terry the bodyguard pales at the thought, the five are mad for it, so we step out into the bright sunlight.

Amazingly, although the pavements are heaving with commuters, no one seems to recognise the band. Perhaps they are too intent on getting home and starting the weekend. We stop at a newspaper stall while Noel buys an evening paper to read about Tony Blair's first day in office. Liam notices a billboard saying that John Major has resigned and stands beside it to have his picture taken. Curiously, the newspaper vendor takes exception to this and asks us to move on.

Two days later an 'exclusive' report will appear in the *News of the World* in which a newspaper vendor claims that Liam tried to steal two placards from her stall and ended up grappling with her. According to the newspaper, Liam hurled foul-mouthed abuse as Patsy Kensit looked on. Apparently there are witnesses to swear what happened. It's a typical example of how tabloid frenzy fills column-inches with fictitious fancy.

We move further up the Euston Road and pause at a bus stop while Jill scans for a suitable location. The two Japanese girls waiting at the stop can't believe their eyes, and start chattering away in high-pitched amazement. One of them delves into a capacious bag and extracts a video camera. Noel and Liam walk straight up to the lens and hamming it up for all they are worth. When they return to Japan, the girls will have an exclusive holiday movie the envy of all their friends that will guarantee Euston Road a mention on the places-most-likely-to-spot-pop-stars list.

Jill returns to the bus stop with news that she has decided how to photograph the band. She instructs them to cross the road so that she can shoot them from afar, amid the rush-hour traffic. Terry's eyebrows disappear off the top of his forehead as he looks at what must be one of the busiest intersections in London. You can almost see the headline crossing his mind: Oasis wiped out as juggernaut swerves out of control.

Amazingly, the occasion passes without incident. Nobody appears to recognise the band. Perhaps nobody expects to bump into five pop millionaires in a seedy, designer-free area. Noel thinks it's a hoot and gestures rudely towards Jill's camera.

Time is wearing on and Bonehead is anxious to make his departure. He has to travel south of the river to pick up his car in order to drive back home to Manchester for the weekend; Alan is heading off in the same direction. Guigs has a splitting headache and is itching to get home to a darkened room. Liam is rubbing his hands at the prospect of a visit to the pub, while Noel, having stayed up all night mastering the album, wants to go home to bed.

It's Friday night, the end of the week. It's been a momentous one. A new government is in power, a new Oasis album is in the can. The band have been reunited and, thirty years on from their heroes, The Beatles, they too have embarked on a magical mystery tour, albeit slightly less psychedelic.

Life is about to get interesting . . .

WAS THERE THEN

IN THE STUDIO

On Friday September 13, 1996, the story that dominated front-page headlines in both the tabloid and broadsheet press was one that sent thousands of fans into despair: Oasis had split up.

'Blowasis' trumpeted the *Sun*, claiming that after a fight in North Carolina, Noel and Liam had axed the band. The story was echoed on television and radio, with only the *Daily Mirror* proclaiming that news of their demise was much exaggerated.

According to reports, the brothers had come to blows during an almighty row that erupted two-thirds of the way through a troubled American tour. Their ninth visit to the States in less than two years had started inauspiciously when Liam decided to stay behind in England, moments before their plane took off for Chicago, to help his fiancée Patsy Kensit search for their new home. It was more important for him to be happy, he said, than to care about upsetting American fans with his non-appearance.

Although the band soldiered on for the first few dates with Noel on vocals, reviews and ticket sales were disappointing. When Liam flew out to join the others a few days later, Noel's resentment at his brother's lack of commitment simmered dangerously until the fateful night in Charlotte when he cancelled the gig and, following a five-hour hotel summit meeting with the rest of the band, the remainder of the tour. He took the first Concorde out of New York and arrived in London, tight-lipped and grim-faced, less than twenty-four hours later.

The amount of space devoted to the incident by the British press was indicative of the band's stature in the UK. Psychologists analysed the symbiotic relationship between the brothers; youth commentators composed elegies to the band's demise and cartoonists had a field day with the permutations of 'Wonderbrawl'.

Outside Noel's St John's Wood house, camera crews from all over the globe gathered like pins to a magnet, hoping to catch sight of him. Major world events went unnoticed as the obsession with tracking down the Gallaghers snowballed beyond belief. Once, when we had been discussing music, Noel had said to me, 'It's entertainment, you know, just like turning on the telly. Nobody should worry about whether

→ p34

Jill: This is one of my favourite photographs of Liam, and I know it's one of his as well. When Noel decided he didn't want to do the band shot outside the Abbey Road Studios, I thought I'd go along to photograph the wall all the same. Then Liam arrived and I asked him if he would stand there and he did. I only shot two frames and this one has such attitude.

Abbey Road 10/96

Jill: I only saw Guigs working a few times at Abbey Road. He likes to work privately, standing by the mixing desk. So I was ejected to Studio 2 and this is me looking into the control room while Guigs does his bit.

Jill: These pictures were taken in Studio 2 at Abbey Road. It's an incredibly inspiring room. It's got a wonderful wooden floor and it was bathed in a beautiful light and obviously the fact it was the Beatles' studio adds weight to the atmosphere. It's an enormous space, which contrasts with the mixing-desk area which is really quite small.

I wasn't there very often during the first few days of recording but Oasis would go in there just to sit and play Beatles' records. It was their way of paying homage.

I was also not there on the occasion that, rumour has it, sleeve designer Brian Cannon took off all his clothes and danced naked in Studio 2! Luckily for him, there's no photographic evidence to back this up!

Jill: I was asked to do this band shot at Abbey Road because of all the media furore that was going on at the time. They'd cancelled the American tour and the papers were saying that they'd split up, so we needed some shots to show they were a working unit.

We were going to do the shot outside the studio in Abbey Road itself, by the wall of graffiti, and then I got this message back from Noel saying 'We're not going to be Japanese tourists.' So we decided to do it in the studio.

Bridge 3
AND ROUND THIS TOWN YOU'T CEASED TO BE
THAT'S WHAT YOU GET FOR SLEEPING
WITH THE ENEMY
WHERE ANGELS FLY YOU WON'T PLAY
I GUESS YOUR GONNA TAKE THE BLAME FOR
CH. 3
MY BIG MOUTH, MY BIG NAME
I'LL PUT ON MY SHOES WHILE I'M WALKING
SLOWLY DOWN THE HALL OF FAME
INTO MY BIG MOUTH YOU COULD FLY A PLANE
I'LL PUT ON MY SHOES WHILE I'M WALKING
SLOWLY DOWN THE HALL OF FAME
SLOWLY DOWN THE HALL OF FAME
SLOWLY DOWN THE HALL OF FAME
SLOWLY DOWN THE HALL OF FAME
SLOWLY DOWN THE HALL OF FAME
SLOWLY DOWN THE HALL OF FAME

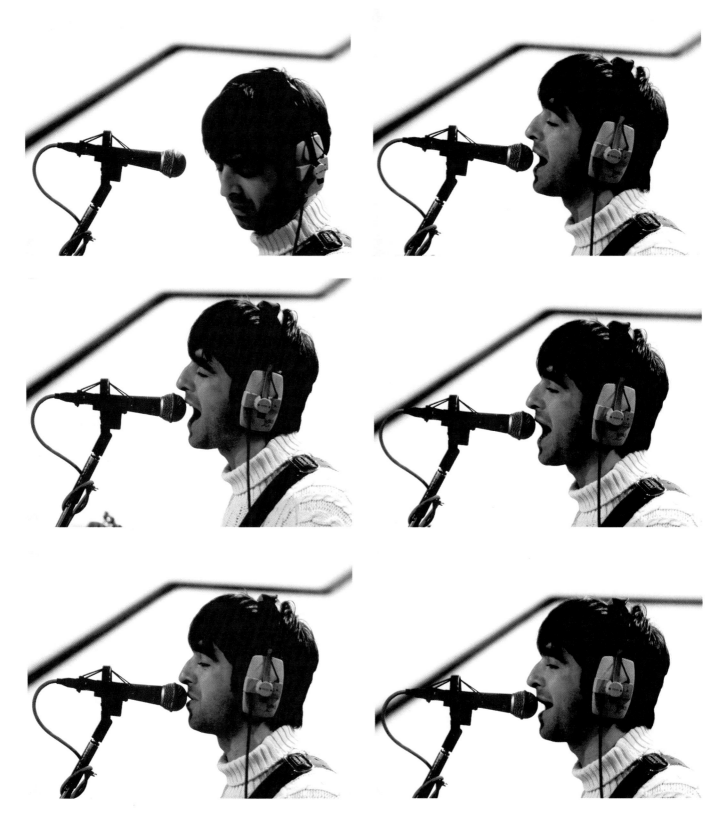

it's important or not. You shouldn't even think about it. If it makes you feel good, if it makes you want to jump up and down, if it makes you cry, just do it. Don't worry about it.' Wherever he was, even though this was a crisis point, I knew he would be amused by all the fuss.

Jill Furmanovsky greeted the news of the Oasis split with disbelief and acceptance. 'I wasn't sure what was going on, but if they had called it a day it wouldn't really have surprised me, having witnessed so many blow-ups with them. I'd been due to join them later on that American tour and I did have a pang of regret when I realised that it might have come to a premature end.

'Pretty soon, my next-door neighbour was ahead of anything I knew. I hadn't a clue what was going on, but he works for the *Daily Mirror* so he was able to give me up-to-date news, although at one point he thought I had the whole band hidden in my flat!

'I went down to St John's Wood to walk around and see the press frenzy for myself, and I couldn't believe the amount of fuss that was being generated. The whole of the High Street was packed with members of the press and their accoutrements, including aerials reaching up to the sky, satellite dishes and television cameras. There were crews filming on Noel's doorstep, bumping into each other, making reports that basically said there was nothing new to report, while little old St John's Wood ladies were being forced off the pavement with their shopping baskets by journalists intent on nailing the big scoop.

'There's a tremendous amount of unpredictability that runs through the band, and that's the hardest part to deal with. It's like walking on a tightrope, although, as their spokesman Johnny Hopkins says, you wouldn't want it predictable. The predictable thing would be that Oasis would have split up by now because that's what everyone expected of them. He's right when he says that what people don't realise is it's *because* they're so unpredictable that they're still together.'

While the world deliberated whether Oasis were no more, Noel Gallagher had made a decision. The band would forget about touring and get to work on their third album, ahead of schedule. But first there was some serious talking to be done.

Although they'd reached breaking-point before, this was without doubt the most serious crisis Oasis had faced. Following the euphoria of the huge Loch Lomond and Knebworth gigs earlier in the year, they should have toured the States on a high. Instead it had all ended in tears.

'When that tour was cancelled, and Noel and Liam disappeared, the press went crazy trying to find them,' says Furmanovsky. 'What actually happened was they were picked up separately at the airport and whisked away to a secret destination in the country: I think the idea was that they should sit down and talk because it had been a falling out of monumental proportions that had caused this tour to end.'

The next thing Jill heard, Oasis had booked into Abbey Road. If any place could inspire them, surely this was the place. Loaded with Beatles'

connections, the studios offered benevolent ghosts to heal the rift – but this wasn't to be.

'Initially the atmosphere in there was pretty depressing,' Jill recalls. 'During the time they were there, the band worked separately. I never saw Liam in there if Noel was working, and vice versa. I think it was deliberate. They were giving each other space. But still I wondered what had gone down between the two.

'Then, one night when Liam was in on his own, he told me what had happened. He said that when he was picked up from the airport, he was met by bodyguards, who shoved him into the back of a van that took him to who knows where. The van drove for miles, and every time he asked where they were going, the driver wouldn't tell him.

'Eventually they stopped near a cemetery and when Liam looked out the window he thought, "Bloody hell, I'm going to be murdered!"'

In the event it was nothing quite so dramatic – or final. Noel was holed up at a friend's home, safe from the prying eyes of the press. He wanted to talk to his brother, to see if their relationship – personal and professional – could be saved.

Although they resolved their problems sufficiently to start work on the new album, relations were strained for a good part of the Abbey Road sessions of *Be Here Now*. It was only some way through recording, when Liam was busted for possessing cocaine, that the vibes between the brothers improved, because Noel had offered moral support. While the move into Abbey Road was a positive start, it was all the same a shaky one. And there were external pressures, too.

'Half the problem was because Abbey Road is pretty central,' Jill observes. 'There was always somebody or other dropping into say hello and it ended up being a distraction. I was suddenly informed that the band was relocating to a residential studio in the country.'

With *Be Here Now*, Noel Gallagher had made a conscious decision to take his time with the recording process. *Definitely Maybe*, in spite of being recorded twice over, in Wales and Cornwall, was still made relatively quickly for a debut album. The fact that the album was ever completed had been a source of wonder to him, and not just because of its turbulent recording history. As Noel told me from Cornwall, four-fifths of the band were in danger of being wiped out before the album was even released. 'At the moment we're recording in a studio that's in the middle of an estuary and those mad fuckers are going off canoeing in the middle of every night,' he had said. 'We're beyond rock'n'roll.'

With the multi-platinum follow-up, *(What's The Story) Morning Glory?*, the band allocated four weeks in their schedule to put down their new songs. It was a confident gesture, given the problems faced with their first album, let alone the pressure often described as 'second-album syndrome'. Confounding their critics, Oasis completed their new offering in less than three weeks.

Jill: When they first started recording the album, Noel and Liam had been working separately at Abbey Road. Then one night, very shortly after Liam had been busted for possessing cocaine, a bunch of us went for a drink. Noel had been very supportive of him during that crisis and you could see that there was a warmth between them that had previously been lacking. Whenever I saw them in the studio after that they seemed to be fine. This picture was taken on that night and you can see there's been some sort of reconciliation.

If *Morning Glory* was a step away from the fuck-you, in-your-face bad boy rock of *Definitely Maybe*, *Be Here Now* is giant leaps ahead of its predecessor.

What seems so uncanny now is that, shortly after releasing *Definitely Maybe*, Noel predicted to me how he envisaged album number three; 'If we just let ourselves become a run-of-the-mill band, I think we'll just get bored with it. We know we can't write another album like the one we've just done because that would be too easy. We've got to use other musicians and different instruments and try to emulate The Beatles as much as possible to keep it interesting. We've got to keep stepping it up.'

He has remained true to his word. As his songwriting skills have become more honed, so too has his vision of how his compositions should be arranged. The fact that Oasis have made millions from their first two albums means that they can afford the best studio space, the best support system and, most important, as much time as they need to get it right. *Be Here Now* reflects his vision – although whether it also reflects his now-dismissed opinion that he couldn't see the band going beyond three albums remains to be seen. Noel says that he is 'still thinking about it.'

With the album being recorded in three phases, at three different locations, it also fell into three different moods. Abbey Road was important for setting the album in motion. Ridge Farm, a residential studio in Surrey, with its dogs and inglenooks and rustic charm, was a place for Noel to finalise his list of songs and for the band to reconvene. But it was in Air Studios, during the final phase, that the band were to be most productive.

Air Studios is an inspiration in itself. Never mind the innovative equipment that it offers, the place alone sets the imagination alight. A former ecclesiastical building, it was bought by Beatles producer George Martin some years ago and restored to its former glory, at the same time transforming it into one of the most comfortable, up-to-the-minute recording studios in the world. Tucked behind elegant – but impenetrable – wrought-iron railings, it perches at the brow of a hill in leafy Hampstead.

For Furmanovsky, as a photographer, working with the band in the studio presented new challenges. 'I hadn't worked with them before during the process of recording and it required very much a different approach,' she explains. 'When I'm onstage photographing them live, I'm capturing a performance. But in a recording studio, I'm chronicling them during a fluid creative process that should not be interrupted or disturbed. More than ever, I have to make myself invisible and not prove to be a distraction.'

'When I first went into Abbey Road, I felt like a bit of an intruder. So I just took my time and didn't shoot unless I thought it was necessary, which gave them time to get used to me being there. By the time I went down to Ridge Farm, it was a very different vibe. For a start it was a residential studio, so it was a much more laid-back atmosphere, and it was in the dead of winter so it had an otherworldly tinge to it. Plus I went down with Marcus Russell, their manager, and that was useful for easing me in again.'

For Noel Gallagher, the weight of being composer and orchestral arranger, musician and co-producer is considerable. A self-confessed control freak, he will often re-record pieces he previously deemed acceptable. Meticulous and demanding – as much of himself as of his fellow band members – his working methods are the complete antithesis of his brother's.

If Noel's role in the studio is to be on top of everything at all times, Liam's is to let rip with abandon. Every song is a performance to him: when he shuts his eyes he is transported to a stage in front of 125,000 revved-up punters. In Air Studios, the much-improved atmosphere between the brothers inspired his best work. And when Liam is happy, he likes to party.

Being an instinctive performer, he likes to surround himself with an audience. There were nights in Air Studios when he played to the gallery, whether it was to Teenage Fanclub, who were treated to an hour-long mimed rendition of every song on the album, or during a take for backing vocals to 'All Around The World' when he was joined by a rabble-rousing chorus of comrades. 'A quiet night in with the boys' as Noel describes such occasions.

During the mass recording session for the 'All Around The World', Noel had intended to be present to make his contribution. He'd been in the studio earlier that day, supervising the orchestra who'd been working in the large studio. When they had dispersed, he'd gone for a short break. When it came to heading back up to Air Studios, for once he couldn't be bothered. 'So I sent Meg instead. I went off to watch the Prince Naseem fight, and then I went out with him after it and got completely trashed!'

Compared to the uneasiness of Abbey Road and the hibernation vibe that emanated from Ridge Farm, the atmosphere at Air Studios was a shot in the arm. The time to stop faffing about had come, and as a unit Oasis was more productive than it had been for months. They were back on track.

For the majority of bands, recording is an intricate, intimate and ultimately private experience. Given the crises that haunted Oasis during this period, it wouldn't be unreasonable to expect them to close ranks even more. Yet, apart from producer Owen Morris, manager Marcus Russell and of course the band, Jill found herself the only person to have consistently witnessed the making of *Be Here Now*. A mark of the respect in which she is regarded, she was granted the ultimate tribute of being permitted to remain in the control room.

Ridge Farm 12/96

Jill: This was taken on a day when Liam wasn't about. The others were watching television or playing snooker in another part of Ridge Farm. I hadn't seen Noel for a while so I crept off to the back entrance of the studio. I heard this acoustic guitar which was very, very enticing and, sure enough, it was Noel working out part of a new song. He carried on and on and on, lost in what he was doing. He was completely alone in that beautiful wooden barn. It was very moving. I sat quietly where he couldn't see me, and there I stayed for about fifteen minutes until I felt like I was spying. Then I made my presence known.

Jill: By the time I took this picture, producer Owen Morris had become accustomed to having me around. He'd been a bit suspicious of me to start with. Owen is quite fierce: I think you have to be to control that mob!

Liam was doing the warm-up for 'Do You Know What I Mean' and I was wondering whether it would be possible to shoot in the same room, because I was worried that the clicking of the shutter might be picked up on the recording. I asked Owen's advice and he said he didn't think it would be a problem, so I decided to try it out during the run-through. The next thing I knew, we were on to the take!

Because there wasn't much available light, I shot it on something like an eighth of a second. All the instruments are sharp but there's a lot of movement in Liam because of the time exposure. His feet are still but his body is blurred because he moves himself forwards and backwards from the microphone to get the effects.

It was a very powerful performance and he was really mad for it, to use his own term; he was really steaming to do it. It was the only vocal he did in Ridge Farm and once he'd finished he knew he'd done a really great job.

Hearing that extraordinary voice on its own without the backing track was awesome. I felt enormously privileged to have witnessed that.

Jill: This picture says to me that Liam knew he'd cracked it. He was leaving the studio and there was such a look of satisfaction on his face. It's a snap, done on a Snappy Snaps camera. I always carry one with me. Another photographer might leave out a picture like this but in the context of story-telling it doesn't really matter what method you use because you've captured the moment.

Jill: This session was done in the farm's snooker and TV room where the band were watching *Conan the Barbarian*! I'd turned it into a photographic studio using a sheet from one of the bedrooms upstairs for a backdrop, and a tungsten light. It was really just an experimental thing, just to see what came out of it. The whole thing took just half an hour. In studio situations I always work quickly because it's such a false environment. You can't hold a pose indefinitely otherwise it becomes just that – a pose, not a portrait. I always try to set the shot up completely so that the subject can walk in and walk out – click, click, click – within a matter of minutes.

Air Studios 02/97

Norman Blake, Teenage Fanclub: We were in Air Studios mixing our album SONGS FROM NORTHERN BRITAIN and one night we bumped into Liam downstairs. We'd met a few times before so after we exchanged how are you's, he said, 'Why don't you come and hear some of our stuff?' We went down to their studio, he cracked open loads of beers and then he started playing back the songs. Liam was really getting into it; he was singing at full throttle and playing air guitar. The minute one song finished he'd bang on another one, without any time for us to comment on the one we'd just heard! He was really excited, urging us to check out this guitar or listen to that bit. They'd hired this massive PA and he had it cranked up to full volume. It was a wild, wild night and he gave a great performance. We were all pretty astounded. He was really nice, a good host. Great fun. Before that night I wasn't so sure he was a star but now I know he's got what it takes.

Wimbledon 1
Manchester United 0

Jill: For most of the time during the making of BE HERE NOW, I had complete access. But when something personal was going on within the band, Owen Morris would indicate to me that I should go away. These pictures were taken during a hiatus in recording when one of the others had some crisis to deal with, and I think it shows the strain.

49

Jill: When Noel saw this he said
to me, 'Now there's a person
who's satisfied with his life and
his career.' I think that says it all.

George Martin & Noel Air Studios 02/97

George Martin: **I consider Noel Gallagher to be the finest songwriter of his generation.**

Jill: I love these. They're all of Liam singing 'All Around The World'. It was towards the end of the period of time at Air Studios and they'd had an orchestra working on a song earlier in the day. Noel had been in too, but he was so tired that when it came to just doing the choruses he sent Meg instead!

It was obvious it was going to be a party night. Brian Cannon and his mates arrived; I think the call went out generally for anybody who could do backing vocals to make themselves available. The Verve's Richard Ashcroft came specially [see previous page]. It went on and on into the night and many a pint was downed. At one point I remember Liam throwing up in the studio and then just carrying on. I'd gone out to find him a bucket!

Liam Gallagher: This was wild. I really enjoyed doing it, I'm mad for it. I had a brilliant time. It's no different from performing, I love it.

(L-R) Alexandra, Brian Cannon, Dave, Owen & Liam
Air Studios 02/97

Owen Morris, producer:
**The album sounded great then,
fuelled by twelve pints of lager!**

ALL AROUND THE WORLD

ON THE ROAD

The Oasis touring machine has become a vast, sprawling monster. If you're going to play to 125,000 people in one go, you need more than a few lights and amp stacks. The more equipment you have, the more roadies you need to assemble it and the more lorries it takes to transport it all. Nothing is as simple as the beat-up van of old that Bonehead used to drive, when he doubled up his role of rhythm guitarist with that of tour manager.

The speed of this metamorphosis has been meteoric. In the late summer of 1994, Oasis were playing tiny, out-of-the-way venues like the Buckley Tivoli in north Wales. Compare that to Knebworth, less than two years later, for which 5 per cent of the British population applied for the 250,000 tickets: the two gigs consumed the same amount of electricity that the whole of Milton Keynes normally uses in an entire day.

As any band or person who has travelled with Oasis will verify, being on the road injects you into a strange bubble in which you are cut off from the rest of the world. You are absolved of any responsibilities, save for getting to the hotel check-out desk by the appointed hour and walking out onstage every night to play to yet another audience. You don't have to worry about how you're going to get there, where you're going to stay, or where you'll eat after the show. Normal everyday things like paying electricity bills and feeding the cat are no longer relevant to your life. In Liam's case, this extends to packing his bags: the management offices are long-used to phone calls from puzzled hotel staff, enquiring if Mr Gallagher realises he has checked out as he has left behind a number of clothes, shoes and toiletries, turning his room into the equivalent of a rock'n'roll Marie Celeste. Fellow band mates and road crew become your family and, although major events are still reported in newspapers and television bulletins, it's as though time has stood still, or as if the rest of the world doesn't exist.

As the miles clock up on the odometer, the stereo is an essential diversion, blasting out band favourites such as the Beatles' *White Album*. Everyone joins in, singing at the top of their voices. To listen to their enthusiastic banter in between songs – 'Check this one out!', 'This has got to be the best song ever' – one forgets they've played it hundreds of times already.

For Oasis, the tour bus has become a sacred ship. When they first progressed to decent vehicles, Noel would extend the invitation to get on the bus to those he felt might liven up proceedings. But those days have long since passed. Travelling is tiring enough without the added distraction of having to entertain guests – no matter how much they are liked. Touring is no longer a novelty; it's a gruelling part of the job.

In the early days, before their first assault on America, Liam and Guigs were scathing of anyone who remotely moaned about the perils of being on tour. 'I can't stand these groups who whine on and on about how tough life is on the road,' proclaimed Guigs on the eve of their American debut. 'If they don't like it, they shouldn't do it.'

'Yeah,' added Liam, working up to one of his infamous spouts. 'All these people moaning about their health. If I die in two years I won't care because I'll have done it, seen it, lived it, know what I mean? What's the point of going to bed early and cutting down on your fags and beer?'

Nowadays, with the reality of nine American tours behind them, each would admit that, while the ninety minutes onstage is still vital, they are less keen on the other twenty-two and a half hours of the day. Noel Gallagher, on the other hand, having been a roadie for The Inspiral Carpets for a number of years before Oasis took over his life, had graduated with the equivalent of an MA in How To Deal With The Worst Parts Of Being In A Band, and consequently was armed with foreknowledge of the horrors ahead.

'Let's see after four weeks in America whether they're still jovial when they've got no clean clothes and they leave them in the laundrette and then some fucker runs off with them,' he said at the time. 'I've seen it all before so I know it can be really good fun, and if you write it all down it looks great – but have you sat on a plane for sixteen hours? The reality of it all is totally unglamorous.'

'For that hour onstage, that's what it's all about. I'd go through anything for that, I'd walk over hot coals. But all that other shit – it's evil, man.'

Although the stakes might have improved considerably since then – first-class plane travel, five-star hotels, someone else to take care of mundanities – the fact remains that touring is a curate's egg. Ask any member of them what they remember about the long, American tours and they'll reply, 'Fuck all.'

'I'm not being rude or anything,' Liam will proffer, 'but it's all a blur.' And it's not just America – it's everywhere. It's Patsy Kensit, with her self-confessed memory of an elephant, who helpfully jogs his memory. When your life has fast-forwarded at maximum warp factor, there's little time to stop and savour the high points. It's interesting to note that, when faced with photographs of backstage rooms or overseas photo-sessions, the ones that prompt Liam's memory are always the ones where he was out of sorts with Noel.

'You never know what you're going to encounter when you fly out to meet them,' acknowledges Jill. 'There's always that unpredictable element of danger that is both unsettling and exciting. Even if you've seen them only days before, something might have happened during that time that completely alters the general mood.

'Sometimes it's taken a few hours for me to realise that all isn't well. Everyone's really polite and happy to have you along and that can lull you into a false sense of security, but then you start to pick up nuances that paint an entirely different picture. It can make my job nerve-wracking.'

In America particularly, touring involves a great deal more promotional work than in other territories, which isn't simply confined to press interviews. Noel, having taken on the mantle of band spokesman, is often required to carry out an additional schedule. A loner by nature, these extra responsibilities further separate him from the other band members. While they're sleeping off the night before or indulging in some retail therapy – all members of the band own up to being mad shoppers – more often than not, Noel will be at some radio station exercising his dry wit.

Occasionally he will bring Bonehead with him for light relief. Not for the listeners – but for Noel himself. Radio phone-in shows, which can be a tedious experience as a solo effort, become an entertaining excursion. Whether the Americans understand their sense of humour is another matter entirely. Witness this excerpt from a Californian local station.

DJ: You're listening to Love Line at K-Rock, from Pasadena in Los Angeles, with Ricky Rachman and Dr Drew. If you've got any questions for the guys from Oasis they're here to answer them. And they'll also be hanging out on Rodney's show after this because he's a big fan, he's been playing them for a long time.

Bonehead: Yeah, we know him. Rod Stewart is it?

DJ: Um, something like that.

Noel: Rod the Mod!

DJ: Let's go to some calls right now. Laurie, who's eighteen, say hello to the guys from Oasis.

Laurie: Oh! Hi. I have a problem. I recently got a job at a CD store and my best friend got the job for me. He's gay, but he's afraid that the boss is going to find out, so he's always hugging and kissing me in front of the boss which makes me really uncomfortable. I don't know how to handle it.

DJ: Sounds like he's not gay, Laurie.

Bonehead: Doesn't sound gay to me.

DJ: Maybe that's a great way to pick up chicks.

Bonehead: What makes you think he's gay? I don't think he is. Sounds like he's mad for you, so sack your boyfriend and get off with him. I'm serious, I'm telling you.

Noel: Sue him!

DJ [swiftly changing the subject]: We were talking a little bit earlier about you guys coming from Manchester. Can you guys give me an example of a good American stereotype?

Bonehead: Extremely large sandwiches, triple-decker sandwiches.

Noel: Suing everyone!

DJ: Um, right. Let's have another call. It's Jenny.

Jenny: I have a problem. I have this guy I'm in love with but he keeps breaking up with me. I try to get on with my life and date other guys, then he starts phoning me and I end up taking him back. Then it happens again. What should I do?

Bonehead: Get rid of him!

Noel: Sue him! And buy a really big sandwich! No! Sue him and buy him a Blur album.

Jenny: I'm so depressed.

Noel and Bonehead (in unison): Oh God!

Bonehead: At least you're called Jenny and not Bonehead. Think about me!

DJ (getting slightly rattled): On to the next call. It's AJ. What do you have to say to the guys from Oasis?

AJ: I just want to say I've never met you guys but I read that you're always fighting, so I would just like to ask you not to fight amongst yourselves. (Sounds of slapping and cries of pain ensue in the background. "Aargh! Gerrof!")

DJ: Come clean AJ. What do you know that we don't? What have you been reading? (Noel to Bonehead, sotto voce: You're sacked, mate.)

AJ: I read that they were making a video and one of them threw a Big Mac at the other one's face.

Noel: It was a cheeseburger.

Bonehead: It would have been a Burger King, it wouldn't have been a Big Mac.

Noel: If I'd have been flinging Big Macs mate, you'd have known about it. There were no Big Macs being flung.

Bonehead: Never fling a MacDonald's, man. Burger Kings.

Noel: I tell you what – you want to try Chicken McNuggets because then you get six goes.

AJ: But –

Bonehead: Yeah, curry sauce is better because it stings your eyes man.

Noel: Yeah.

DJ (trying to bring order to proceedings): You know, a lot of bands don't get on with each other and they still make music together. Do you guys ever brawl, does it ever come down to blows?

AJ: Yeah! I've read that! You shouldn't be fighting.

Noel: A few times we fight. Yeah. But that's just me and my brother, that's what brothers do.

Bonehead: Have you got a brother?

AJ: No. I gotta sister, but I don't hit her –

Noel: Well even more reason to fight with her!

AJ: And I read there was some hotel you trashed.

Noel: It's rock'n'roll!

AJ: You guys are really great and I don't want you guys breaking up like Suede.

Noel: Oh we won't break up like Suede. (Conspiratorially) Suede aren't very good, that's the problem. (Sounds of shocked laughter coming from the producer's booth.)

DJ: Thanks, AJ. Now here's Bob, twenty-three, from San Gabriel. Bob, you're on Love Line on the world-famous K-Rock.

Caller: Hello? My name's Tony, actually.

Noel: Tony Ashley?

Caller: Tony.

Bonehead: But Ashley, is that your second name?

Caller: I said Tony actually.

Noel, Bonehead and DJ: Ah, Tony Actually.

DJ: And you thought Bonehead was a tough name to have.

Bonehead: Where does Actually come from? (Silence) I think you're lying.

Noel (in Scouse accent): It's from Liverpool, isn't it?

Caller (exasperated): No, they got my name wrong.

Bonehead: Oh, it's not Tony Actually.

Caller: No! It's Bob Ac-tu-all-y I said! But I'm Tony!

DJ (really getting into it now): So it's Tony Actually, not Bob Actually.

Noel: Good, I'm glad we got that cleared up. Now what's the problem? Is it Pearl Jam? Suede? Blur?

Caller: Pearl Jam sucks. But grunge is cool.

Bonehead: Uuurrgh.

Noel: Can you buy that in MacDonald's, grunge?

Bonehead: Can I have a grungeburger?

→ p83

Jill: I'd driven up to Cambridge to see Oasis at the Corn Exchange. There was a very definite buzz of excitement in the air that you couldn't help but be affected by.

When the band came onstage and did almost nothing I found it baffling. The audience was going berserk and Liam was doing nothing, just sitting on the drum riser when he wasn't singing. He seemed completely disinterested unless he was performing – there was no contact or emotion. I thought, what the hell is this? How could a band that had so little action going on onstage incite so much interest and excitement? But that's what caught my imagination, so I decided to concentrate on this suppressed energy and on Liam in particular. The way he held his hands behind his back, the way he moved his head, the way he stared at the audience was fascinating. And they seemed as mesmerised by him as I was. I sensed a completely different vibe emanating from Noel. I was standing right underneath him and he was very friendly. He would smile from time to time and I felt quite responsive to him, whereas I felt uneasy about going too close to Liam. In fact I shot him with a telephoto lens! It wasn't the music that night that intrigued me, it was the chemistry. There was definitely something going on.

Jill: In October 1995 I flew out to meet them in San Francisco for a day's shooting. They'd travelled in overnight on the tour bus and were absolutely shattered. This photograph, which has been used all over the world, sums up so much for me. I thought here we are, you bunch of schmucks from Manchester, in front of one of the greatest backdrops on earth and all you can do is look bored. Although we still hardly knew one another, I did feel a change had taken place between us. Once they've taken you on and they've decided you're OK, then you can just do your job. Everybody was very professional about doing the shoot which surprised me because they'd come in so wrecked. Everyone's a little dishevelled. These are clothes that have been on the tour bus, although I believe Bonehead made an effort and ironed his shirt! It was also during this photo session that I realised that Oasis had extremely low boredom thresholds and I knew I had to keep it moving if I wanted to guarantee success.

Cleveland 03/95

Jill: What's interesting in this photograph is Liam's demeanour. The band were on another US tour, March '95, and they were refusing to meet the wives of record company executives during the meet-and-greet sessions after every show. They were being extremely rude to everyone who came into the dressing-room – and I mean really rude. I was shocked by their behaviour. But this lady journalist got the time of day because she'd met and interviewed John Lennon. That's all she had to say to enter the inner sanctum.

San Francisco 01/95

Detroit 03/95

Jason Rhodes, Noel's guitar technician: God, I remember this! It was a really cramped dressing-room with two doors, one leading on to the stage and the other on to an alley. Halfway through the set Noel shot offstage because he needed a piss, so I had to hold the door open on to the street while Noel took a leak. Liam was onstage telling the audience his brother had nipped off for a piss.

Jill: These were taken while they were filming a video for 'Wonderwall' and it was clear to me that there was potential to move into other markets. Liam looked so sexy that day. Just look at him – he's a bad boy but he's also a pussycat. Both the brothers are seriously sexy when they make an effort.

Jill: I felt terribly nervous at Earls Court. Outside, the crowds were gathering and inside Noel had surprised the band by presenting them all with scooters he'd bought for them in Italy. They were delighted with their new toys and they were riding them crazily in the cavernous backstage area, very fast. Then it was suggested that we should do a picture outside the venue. Security was very worried at the prospect and we had to have a plan of how we would do this. I wasn't feeling my best that day, and I was apprehensive because I knew I had to get this shot right. It was a one-off, not the sort of thing you'd get a second crack at. The promoter and I went ahead in a limo and cleared the area. On a signal, the band came roaring out from the sides and everybody erupted. I had the camera on motordrive and I shot off two rolls. Luckily they came out perfectly. Looking back, it was terribly exciting; that's the whole point about Oasis. It's nerve-wracking to shoot something that moves as fast as they do.

Rhode Island 03/96

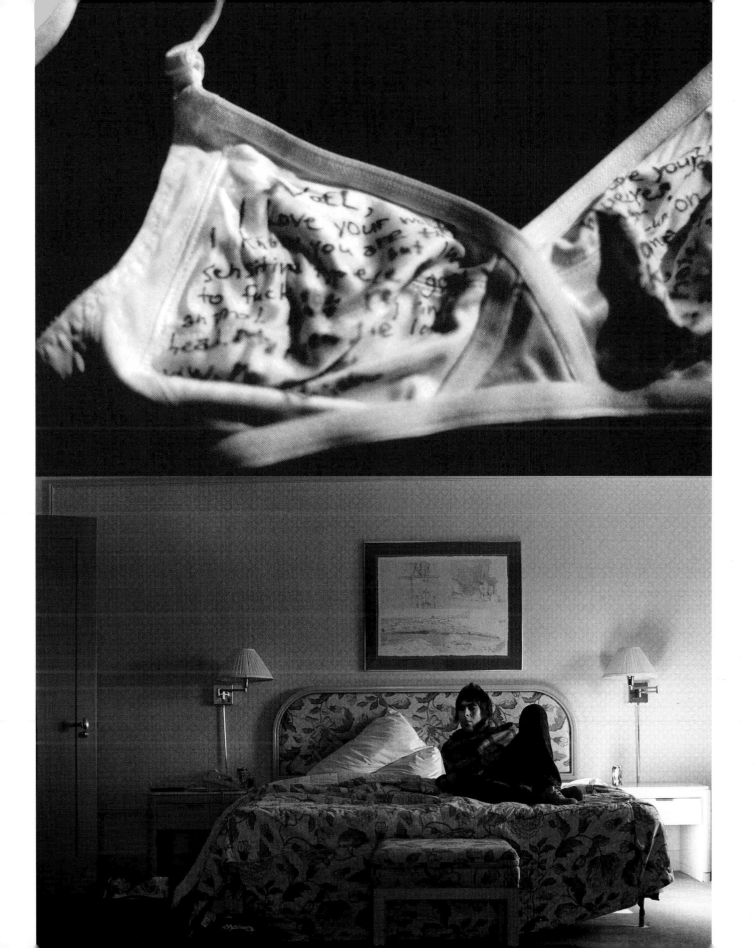

Philadelphia 03/96

80

Philadelphia 03/9[?]

→ p63

Caller: Well...uh...I was just wondering..I hope you guys will give me a straight answer. I was wondering about penis enlargements: what disadvantages are there to it?

Noel: They almost always end up drummers.

While Oasis are recognised as being one of the most significant bands of the decade all around the world, in America this is perhaps less apparent. In Britain, although Noel happily turns up on Jo Wylie's radio show for a chat, it's because he enjoys doing so. In America however, he's prepared to appear on shows that have a fairly small demographic area and be subjected to inane questions because he understands the value of building up the foot-soldiers bit by bit.

The same goes for other promotional exercises. He has been asked to turn up with his guitar at some strange places, but perhaps none quite so unusual as the time he attempted to perform at an outdoor gig – Snowasis – at an upstate New York ski resort in the middle of winter.

'The rest of the band had the day off, but Noel had to fly into New York and from there we had to drive in pretty bad weather to a ski resort,' remembers Jill, who recorded the event with her camera. 'Although we expected it to be cold, the wind-chill factor meant it was about minus 30 degrees, and it was out in the open, which was a bit much.

'Noel played two songs before his hand nearly froze to the guitar fretboard. It took him about half an hour to unbend his fingers. Then we had to take another three-hour journey to Philadelphia – and then he had to do the gig.'

Because he is the hardest-working member of the band, Noel Gallagher feels justified in digging in his heels when he feels his time is being wasted. He refuses to take part in the indignity of what is known in the business as meet-and-greet sessions, where he or the entire the band is expected to attend a reception or have dinner following the gig with key record company staff and their wives. These sessions are seen as a perk to employees but, given that most of the executives are fifty-something baby-boomers, they don't have much in common with five mouthy musicians. This is the corporate aspect of the music industry, and one which holds no appeal for Noel, especially when, during such an occasion, a top executive introduced him as Neil.

It's events like this that make tempers fray, especially when they happen several weeks into the tour. You could almost set your clock to when Liam will spontaneously combust, although he's not the only one who can jump off at the deep end.

As Jill explains, 'On the same tour as Snowasis, Marcus Russell saw Liam spill a drink on Bonehead's jacket and Bonehead took exception to this. "I don't mind you spilling it on my head, but don't you diss my jacket." The next thing they were out scrapping in the snow and someone had to call the bodyguards Terry and Kevin to separate them. Five seconds later they were hugging.'

Scraps like these are more likely to occur when the number of gigs still to be played exceeds those already done, in spite of having been on the road for weeks. The trouble with the sheer geographical mass of the States is that it takes so long to cover, so it's not as though the problem will disappear.

The trouble is, the Americans don't know what to make of Oasis which, for the band, makes touring a bit like banging their head against a brick wall. The same thing happened with Led Zeppelin, who were first regarded as Antichrists who played a witches' brew of blues and heavy rock. Oasis, with their sometimes oafish behaviour and melodic rock appear to be just as difficult for the Americans to define.

'To some extent, I think America is a bit baffled by Oasis,' says Jill. 'Noel's acoustic set, for example – the band just stop, it looks like the show might be finished, and then the stool comes on. During a gig in Rhode Island, when he was doing his solo bit, the audience was vibed up to rock'n'roll. This boot came sailing out of the crowd and hit him on the side of the head and then fell onto his guitar.

'Noel just walked off, and Liam came back on and went absolutely berserk, screaming at the audience that Noel was a great songwriter and that they should pay him more respect.

'I think it was simply that American audiences haven't quite twigged that Oasis aren't like the local bands who were supporting them – rock bands who still get down on their knees and throw guitar poses.

'To some degree, their presentation has an element of menace. Liam seems as much influenced by John Lydon as John Lennon, and Noel is almost folksy – it's an odd combination for a US audience.'

Noel Gallagher says that, because the American market is so defined, with specialist radio stations catering to a narrow band of music-lovers, it's more difficult to cross over into different markets. If you're perceived as one thing, people are less willing to accept you in any other form.

'The thing about America is they say to you – "So you guys play Les Paul? So you're a rock band? But you haven't got long hair. So you're not a rock band" – and when we reply that we're a rock'n'roll band, they look totally confused,' Noel says. 'They try and pigeonhole everything. If it's not one particular thing they don't want to know and this is why Primal Scream will never make it there, because here's this band who are white, they're Scottish, yet they sing in black American accents. They play guitars, they're a live band, but they've got a drum machine and a black singer. They play rock music that is also dance music and the Americans can't sell that because they can't put it in a rack in Tower Records. Do they put it in Rock or Pop or Dance or Soul or Blues? Because it's all of those things. So when we try and tell them we're a rock band, but not in the sense that Guns N' Roses are, it confuses them. We're something else. We're an English rock band, whatever that means.'

One ploy which has gone some way to redressing the balance has been to support musicians to whose fans Oasis might appeal – such as Neil

→ p86

New York 03/96

Young in 1996 or U2 in summer 1997 – and, by the same token, have up-and-coming hipsters support them, like Beck. Whatever, the list of names adding their seal of approval is growing steadily.

It was in this manner that the connection was made between Noel and one of his heroes, Burt Bacharach. In 1994, Noel was raving about him, when few others admitted to seeing the appeal.

'I just love his music and when I tell other people they say, you're taking the piss,' he said then. 'But if you're talking songs, he's up there with John Lennon. The thing about him is he's a great songwriter. I'd never heard of him, then somebody played me an album and I knew every song on it. I was going, are these all written by the same guy? I was amazed.'

When Bacharach heard of his latest fan, he checked out Oasis for himself and liked what he heard. 'It's really good listening,' the master told *Mojo* magazine. 'It's not hard for me to go through that tape because I found it pretty creative. They get a very wide sound, the tracks feel very good. Liam's voice is unusual.'

During one of Oasis's early spring tours in 1996, Bacharach's management got in touch with their management company Ignition in London and a meeting was set up between the two musicians. Later that year, when Bacharach was scheduled to play a concert in London, he invited Noel to make a guest appearance to sing one of his songs. But what with the schedules of both artists and the actions of unhelpful hotel staff the pair only managed to meet less than twenty-four hours before the gig.

Christine Biller, an American who works for the band, was sitting behind Noel. 'We watched the first half of Burt's performance and he just couldn't settle. He was so fidgety and nervous! But he needn't have worried because he was so brilliant when he went up to sing 'This Guy's In Love With You'. It was perfect. I was so proud.'

Now that Liam and Noel have become two of the most recognised faces on the planet, their chances of anonymity are almost gone, and with it the opportunity to turn up unaccompanied in bars or wherever else they like. It's something that affects Guigs, Alan and Bonehead too, albeit to a lesser degree. In a sense, they have all traded freedom for fame.

In some ways it's hard to imagine, so obscene are the amounts of money and the levels of success they have achieved. But although Oasis are able to enjoy the trappings of wealth and tolerate the need for bodyguards, what's reassuring is the fact that they as people maintain the same values and seem essentially the same blokes they were before.

Friend and sleeve designer Brian Cannon has been around since the beginning, and he too notes a sea-change in the band. 'It used to be a lot wilder in the old days,' he says. 'When it gets to the size of Loch Lomond, they're living in a goldfish bowl. The security around them is intense. Nothing seems to get damaged any more. Bonehead no longer throws stuff out of windows and, believe me, I've been there in the past to see it.'

Noel has said that he doesn't want to repeat the stature of the Loch Lomond or Knebworth gigs. 'Bigger than big,' he called them, and how much bigger can you go after that?

Which makes one speculate whether their touring days are over. When Liam looks over Jill's live shots, he almost drools. 'Mad for it,' he says. 'I miss that.'

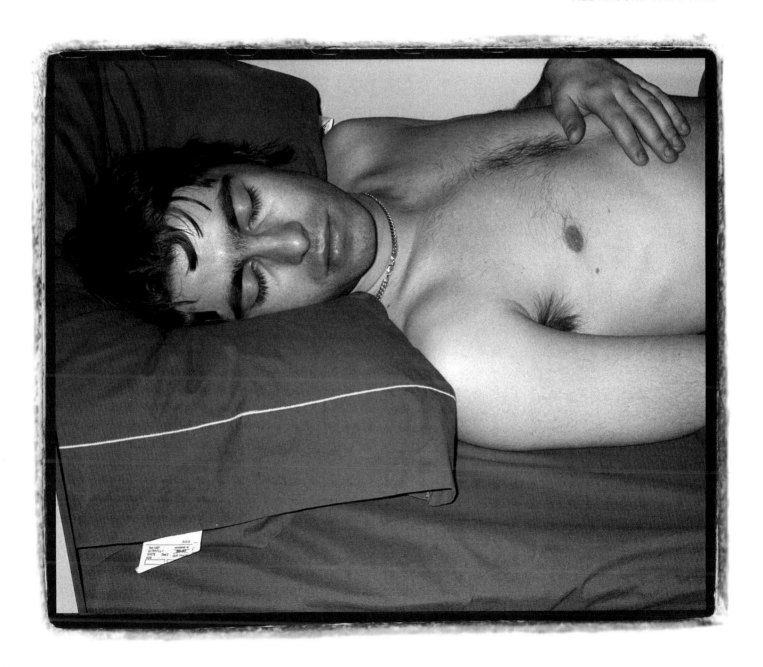

Noel Gallagher: We were in the hotel in Dublin and I could hear this commotion going on outside. I walked across the room and pulled back the curtain, and I could see all these fans going wild. Fucking amazing. It's one of the best sights I've ever witnessed. I don't think many people went to school that day.

Daniela Soave: Liam has a rare respect for songwriters he admires. Even if he doesn't like a band as a whole, if there's a song that has touched him in any way, he's passionate about that piece of music and its composer. I saw this for myself one night at my house, when a whole crowd of us had come back after some mad party in town. He asked if I had NIRVANA UNPLUGGED, which threw me a little as I didn't think it was the kind of thing he'd request. He wanted to hear 'Jesus Don't Want Me For A Sunbeam', which he used to play every day on the tour bus. When I told him it was my friend Eugene Kelly who wrote the song, Liam's eyes welled up. He went up to Eugene – who hadn't a clue about the conversation we'd just had – and shook his hand, before rushing out of the room overcome with emotion. I love the fact the Liam's so affected by the power of music – it's why he's the best singer.

Jill: Everybody wanted to have their photograph taken with Burt Bacharach. They were so happy to be in his company. After the gig, there was a party backstage and Noel kept urging me to take a snap of Kate Moss with Burt, or one with Burt and Noel's friends Phil and Coyley. I was bemused because for me Burt Bacharach epitomises Radio 2 music so I was surprised that they all thought it was so top. Noel did sing beautifully though!

Jill: Creation Records had asked me to come down to a west-London hotel because they were giving the band presents. First of all they gave the others expensive watches and then they took Noel outside. Parked by the kerb was a chocolate Rolls Royce. He was gobsmacked by the whole affair. I thought it was hilarious because he couldn't drive and you can't park in Camden, where he was living at the time, anyway. This picture, with the writer Paul Mathur, really sums up the mood.

Jill: In July '96 the band took over the Birmingham NEC to rehearse for their summer shows at Knebworth, Loch Lomond and Cork. It was another period when Liam was being pretty manic, bonkers even. On the day I was there he didn't sing. John Squire, the ex-Stone Roses guitarist, came down because they'd asked him to play at the gigs. Noel and Liam were both really touched and chuffed. Squire, being as surly as they are, just arrived and plugged in his guitar without a word, and they rehearsed 'Champagne Supernova'.

These girls are the teenage daughter of an NEC guard and her friends. They'd dressed up to the nines in anticipation of being allowed in, which they were, so they sat and watched. Can you imagine – they had an Oasis show to themselves. This is Liam with them and I was absolutely fascinated because I identified with those girls. I thought what if this had been me with The Beatles at that age, I'd never have ever forgotten that. I can see myself in those girls.

97

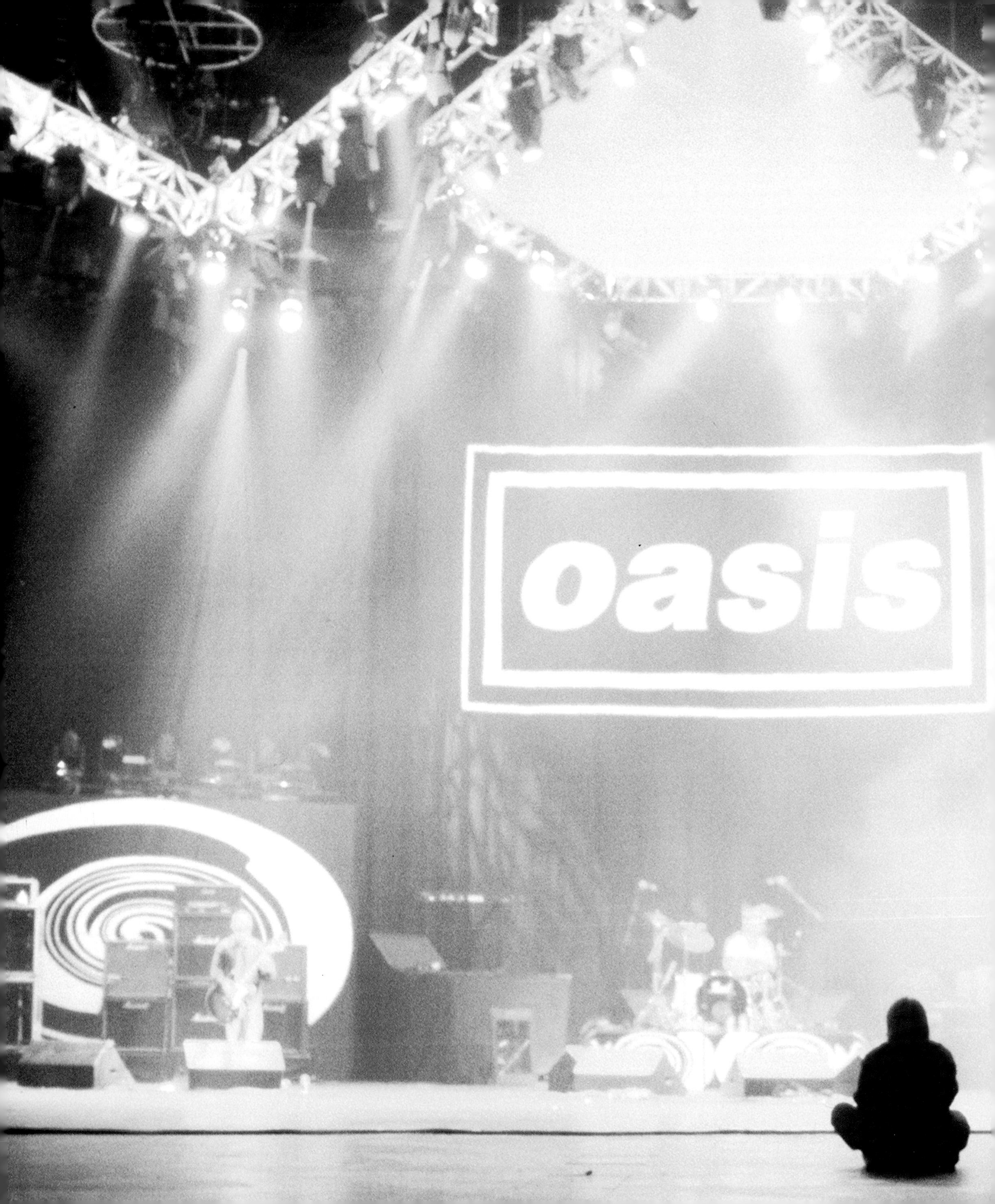
oasis

Birmingham 07/96

ALL TOGETHER NOW

THE BROTHERS GALLAGHER

There is a dark, unfathomable side to Oasis that definitely stems from the strange chemistry between the two brothers. Although he's most likely to be the one who throws huge tantrums or shakes everyone to the core with his unpredictability, Liam is also the one who is most honest about what he feels. Dubbed by the other members of the band 'the Tasmanian Devil', Liam is a bubbling cauldron of conflicting emotions. Noel, by contrast, is cool, critical and clear-cut about how he perceives the world. Coming from polar opposites of the spectrum, it's difficult enough to exist in the same family, let alone function together in a professional manner.

Add to this the strange foundations of their working relationship. Originally, Oasis was Liam's brainchild. It has been much reported how Noel, having seen the band perform at a local venue, told them that Liam had a definite something but their songs were shite. If he came on board and called the shots, they were destined for great things.

While Noel's prediction came true, it has created a potent dynamic between the two brothers. As in his personal life, Liam professionally seeks approval from his brother. Whether he gets it as often as he would like is another matter entirely. The fact is that the two approach work from very different directions and, as far as Noel is concerned, there's only one correct way – his. As a result, Liam feels his contribution is undervalued. Says journalist Ashley Heath: 'Noel is a great songwriter but Liam changes things from being a very good band into something more than that.'

Never was this more apparent than at the ill-fated *MTV Unplugged* session in 1996. When Liam was unable to sing at the last moment, Noel manfully took over the entire show. As his confidence has grown, so too has his stature as a singer, but even so, he will never be Liam. Those who think Oasis could exist without the younger Gallagher are fooling themselves. Liam adds aggression and passion to Noel's compositions. No one else could deliver Noel's lyrics in quite the same way.

On the one hand, Liam is without doubt the most powerful and instinctive singer of his generation. Those who have heard Noel perform 'Wonderwall' – surely one of the most romantic, bittersweet songs of the decade – will recognise that it's a very different beast in the hands

Jill: All the band members are very fond of their families. This picture of Noel with his mother Peg and his aunties was taken backstage at The Point and you can see how delighted he is.

Jill: Bonehead is more of a party man. He has one of those faces that make you want to laugh – he could have been a comedian. He's emotional in a most un-macho way. He's the person to seek out if you need a hug.

of Liam, who effortlessly transforms it with frightening ease into something more sinister and trenchant.

Noel, conversely, is the master songsmith – the best of his generation, as Liam is so quick to point out – and is also the one who spends hours patiently doing promotional duties that would send Liam off into orbit within minutes. No matter what is going on in his life, he puts the interests of the band first.

Because Noel's the more professional, he's often irked by Liam's unpredictable methods. Noel complains that Liam is disruptive and unfocused, and questions his need to bring friends to the studio to party while they are recording.

But this is how Liam best works. What works for Noel isn't necessarily what works for his younger brother. In photo-sessions Liam has grown tired of the conventional, scowling shot and as a result tries to inject a bit of movement and humour into the frame. Nine times out of ten, these are the ones that are rejected out of hand by Noel. The same goes for the way Liam behaves in the recording studio. For Noel, as performer, composer, arranger and co-producer, making a record is a painstaking process.

Liam, on the other hand, has to come in and sing, and to do that well he needs to create a party atmosphere. Just because Liam's method is so different from Noel's doesn't mean to say it's any less valid – it's just a hell of a lot more anarchic – but Liam is aware of his brother's highly critical stance. This is the reason it works.

Says journalist John Harris of the brothers' relationship: 'The point is, I think they had an unequal relationship to start with. Noel was already writing these amazing songs, but Liam hadn't quite found his vocal feet, which I suppose happened decisively just before *What's The Story*. Back then, he was known chiefly for being this mad, excessive and slightly demonic figure. Now, he's been talked about as one of the best singers this country's ever produced, so the relationship's got this real air of mutual artistic respect. Plus, they're not cooped up in a transit van driving from shitty venue to shitty venue. In those circumstances, even Jesus and John the Baptist would have arguments.'

When the two fall out, it's not just them who are affected by the atmosphere. A cloud hangs over the rest of the band. Those who think that 'the other three' are interchangeable miss the point entirely. Alan, Bonehead and Guigs are as vital to maintaining the chemistry as Noel and Liam, and they often are the ones who smooth troubled waters.

'The other three are incredibly down to earth about all that's happening,' says Jill. 'They know that they're not the ones who are going to have to do interviews and pictures.

'Guigs is so laid-back and gentle and easy. It's nice just to sit in a room with him. He's got very little ego. On one of the American tours, when Noel was off doing Snowasis, Guigs volunteered to take care of Noel's laundry.'

Alan White, with his cheerful, easy manner is a great mood leveller, while sometimes Bonehead is the only one who can take Liam aside in times of tantrums and talk him back down to earth. The same camaraderie is also evident with the Oasis crew. 'They're very close to their crew, and the crew are passionate about them as well', says Jill. 'Margaret Mouzakitis, the tour manager, is a Greek American. Jason Rhodes, the guitar roadie, was with Johnny Marr and New Order. Roger Nowell is the bass man. I hadn't seen that in quite a while, a band so tight with their road crew. After a gig, Noel doesn't spend time in the dressing-room, he goes into the crew production office and sits in there with a beer, while the other four will sit in the dressing-room with wall-to-wall women. Noel isn't that happy around crowds. He prefers a small gathering.'

The family also extends to press officer Johnny Hopkins and manager Marcus Russell. Says Noel of Marcus, 'The amazing thing about Marcus is he doesn't have a contract with any of his bands. He says, "If ever you don't want to work with me you just tell me and we'll call it quits. We don't need any legal shit and if I don't want to work with you, I'll just tell you." '

Jill Furmanovsky believes that one of the reasons that Oasis have stayed together so far has been Russell's calming influence. 'When they cancelled the American tour in September 1996, the way that Marcus handled the situation saved them an enormous amount of money. This shows how astute he is, but it also diffused the situation within the band. I do think he's contributed to their success, because he's always there for them. I think the fact that Noel chose him for his best man at his wedding also shows how much he thinks of him. Truly great management is rare.'

Another stalwart is the designer Brian Cannon, who is responsible for masterminding the Oasis logo and all of their record sleeves. Though Cannon first met Noel when he shared an office building with The Inspiral Carpets, the pair didn't become friends until he started designing for them. 'I wasn't a mate initially,' he says. 'Noel and Liam I'd met before, but I didn't meet the others until a gig at Sheffield University where they were supporting BMX Bandits and 18 Wheeler. But it was through work that our friendship grew, not the other way around. I think the core crowd of friends has remained more or less the same; it hasn't changed just because they've become rich and famous. If anyone's been dropped, usually it's for a good reason.'

To be a member of Oasis is to be in a position envied by thousands all over the globe. And, as for the Gallagher brothers, to have created something so potent is an achievement they're only now beginning to recognise. Perhaps brothers of thirty and twenty-five no longer fight so passionately. Perhaps brothers of that age don't fight at all. Most brothers, however, aren't two-fifths of the biggest band in decades or living in the public eye. Noel and Liam will always have a spiky relationship. They're always going to disagree about something. But with any luck, their (nuclear) fall-out of 1996 has forewarned them of a future without Oasis, a fate neither currently wishes to contemplate.

Jill: There are a lot of women in the crew. The key is that Oasis like women. That's why I'm there. I'm not sure a male photographer would be tolerated in the same way. I think they find men threatening or, if not that, men in authority.

Maggie, their tour manager [above], is a true professional. I was staggered by her. Maggie's in charge of the men. This has made it much easier for me because there's a natural respect for women in the organisation.

Johnny Hopkins, band spokesman: Oasis work well with women, whether it's journalists, photographers, women in their crew or in the management company. You just have to look at how many females are involved in the entire organisation. I know it sounds corny but they all have very strong relationships with their mothers and that's the real key. They also have good relationships with the women they go out with or are married to. I like them to work with women. It makes more sense because it draws a lot more out of them. It puts a much better perspective on things.

Paris 11/95

Jill: I don't know what had been going on between them. It could have been some small comment that sparked things off. Liam spent the evening in the bar with endless vodka and oranges. The MTV awards were being held that evening and there were loads of people arriving – a distraction we didn't need. We arranged to meet at Noel's room and when Liam didn't show up, my heart sank. He'd gone back to the bar straight after breakfast. Yvonne McConaghy, who was assisting me, went to try and coax him out but he flatly refused to go anywhere near Noel's room. He said he'd do the photo session as long as it wasn't in Noel's room, so we got in the bus and he took his drink with him. We stopped off at this bridge and the first thing Liam did was hurl his glass at the side of the bridge. Noel was furious, but I took him aside and said look, it doesn't matter. As long as you stand there I'll catch him in the frame. But Noel was so pissed off, and you can see it in these photos. He is literally gritting his teeth. The body language is incredible. It was awful. You can almost hear the air crackle.

Jill: Even Liam would admit that, in the past, there have been times when he has been grossly unprofessional. But you can't be like that with a band of this level, and Liam has figured this out for himself. I'd say a change has taken place because the music's taken over. Liam wants to do the best he can and all during the making of BE HERE NOW he kept saying that the album's got to be better, we can't stay as we are, we've got to move on. It's a question of respect. It's very hard to respect someone who drops out of things and the difference is that Liam has become professional – or more professional than he was. He hasn't lost his contempt for the business side. To be honest, when I first started working with them I didn't think they'd get this far. Liam can be the sweetest person and that's the side I see most, but there's also a malevolence that's almost tangible, especially when he drinks too much. He has this huge power to upset everything and occasionally he has used this in a very childish way to destroy things. While it's intensely annoying for everyone else, in a perverse way I'm sure it's his way of maintaining his sanity. If you start to take the music business or being rich and famous and being a pop star seriously, then you're in trouble.

Yvonne McConaghy: I'd witnessed some of what went on the night before. Liam had been trying to be friendly with Noel and Noel was giving him a hard time, and that's what started him off on his binge. The impression I got was that Noel had so much power over him.

He seemed very vulnerable that day. He was totally pissed by the time we did that photo session but he was desperately trying to get in with Noel again.

Liam Gallagher: I remember that. I wasn't speaking to him. We hadn't spoken for about two days.

Jill: There were problems with MTV UNPLUGGED. The set was just ghastly, no one liked it. There seemed to be hundreds of people running around all being terribly important, from MTV and the US record company. It was a very important event, but from the band's point of view, because it was sandwiched between Knebworth and the American tour, it was something of a chore.

Liam was poorly that day. He had a bad throat, and during the day he had been resting his voice. As the evening wore on it became apparent that he thought he couldn't sing. There was this business of looking for doctors; the MTV bigwigs and the record company didn't know what was going on and it had to be kept quiet. The tension was enormous. Worse still, Noel didn't know what was going on. Up to the last minute I don't think anyone knew whether Liam would sing or not. Noel of course gave it all he had, and I've met lots of people who thought it was really good. Liam watched it from the balcony, shouting encouragement. Normally you'd think if you were ill you'd be too embarrassed to stay but he was there. The audience noticed him and after the performance they clamoured for him to come down. When he strode on stage the entire auditorium erupted. Everybody thought he'd rallied and was going to sing, even I thought he would. But the whole thing felt so false that I was pleased he didn't.

Liam: Fuck me, I look like a gangster!

CUM ON FEEL THE NOIZE

THE SUMMER OF '96

'**M**an-U won today,' grumbles Liam Gallagher to the 125,000-strong crowd at Knebworth Park. 'How about a very big fucking massive fuck-off boo for Man United?' The crowd complies happily, hissing and booing as if to some pantomime dame. From his side of the stage, Noel surveys the sea of bodies stretching from the barrier in front of him way back into the horizon. 'This is history,' he proclaims, visibly moved. 'I thought it was Knebworth,' Liam interjects.

The crowd erupts as Alan White starts up the beat and Noel's guitar swirls dramatically into 'Columbia'. It's August 11, 1996: the second night of Knebworth, their fourth momentous gig in nine days. Momentous isn't too grand a word: so far, 330,000 people have succumbed to the delicious, rebellious vibe that is Oasis, electrifying every nerve-ending in the process.

This year there has been no Glastonbury, but who the fuck cares when Oasis have put on the best shows of the summer? Each seven-hour extravaganza has boasted a different supporting bill that features the cream of British music: The Charlatans, The Prodigy, Dreadzone, Manic Street Preachers, Kula Shaker, The Chemical Brothers, Ocean Colour Scene, Black Grape, Cast and – since the real ones can't make it – The Bootleg Beatles.

Gallagher senior is right when he describes the event as history. Knebworth 1996 will go down in the record books as the biggest outdoor gigs ever but, more importantly, a generation of music lovers will go to their bath-chairs with searing memories of a moment they never wanted to end. So what if the sound wasn't perfect? Who cares that one day it rained? Fifty years from now, the merest refrain of an Oasis song will catapult the listener back to those heady August days with memories so potent they are almost tangible. That is the real power of music.

Tonight Liam prowls the stage like a sleek panther, conjuring up an alchemist's spell that captivates and controls, altering the mood with a tilt of the head or change of tone. For those who have followed Oasis since the early days, it's a fascinating transformation.

→ p122

→ p114

The first time Liam Gallagher came close to having an inkling of what was to come was in September 1994, when Oasis toured Japan for the first time. Back in Britain, *Definitely Maybe* had become the fastest-selling debut album of all time, their three singles had rocketed into the charts and their gigs, though still modest in size, were sell-out affairs. But all that paled when compared to the bedlam that went down in Tokyo, Osaka and Nagoya, where Oasis found themselves treated like the second coming.

In Japan, Liam was still discovering his power. In those days he was mostly oblivious to the audience, spitting out Noel's lyrics as if he were delivering them from a different, better world. Still coming to terms with the fact he was now living the dream, you'd sometimes catch him start with shock as he'd open his eyes to the frenzy in front of him. Then he'd catch a face in the crowd, wave artlessly and the entire auditorium would erupt.

Contrast that to summer 1996. Liam Gallagher is having it, and having it large. He is mad for it, so mad in fact that at the very first gig at Loch Lomond he rushed onstage before they had time to screen Brian Cannon's opening film. Cannon, it's said, was distraught but, for Liam, the sight of the crowd stretching all the way back up the hill was too much, too enticing, too wild to wait a moment longer. Because now Liam understands what he was put on earth for. This.

This is something he does better than anyone else on the planet. This is where he can look out over a sea of faces, hundreds of thousands of them, and feel at home. This is where it finally makes sense. It sure as hell made no sense before. Because Liam was a star waiting for the world to wake up to him.

Noel, meanwhile, quietly enjoys himself onstage. Sometimes he catches Bonehead or Guigs' attention and a beatific grin spreads over his face. Or you catch him smiling as he loses himself in an intricate guitar burst.

But the moment he really comes into his own is during his acoustic interlude, although this time he's accompanied by the string section. The first time he did this was in Japan, when the promoters asked Oasis to play for an hour and a half. Accustomed only to playing for fifty minutes or so, Noel decided to feature an interlude of stripped-down compositions, to show the audience how his songs are born – 'me, a guitar and a Walkman'. The experiment worked. Now, he says, he will always include this section in live shows.

Just as Liam's voice has become stronger, so too has Noel's and, with that, his confidence in performing alone. This time he gives the *Unplugged* treatment to 'Whatever' – a sweeter, more gentle version than that sung by his brother – 'Cast No Shadow', dedicated as always to the man who inspired it, Richard Ashcroft of The Verve, and 'The Masterplan', which the *Observer* later proclaims to be Oasis's equivalent to 'Stairway To Heaven'.

By the end of the show, the audience has been worked up to fever pitch. We all know it's coming to its conclusion, but nobody wants to

accept this inevitability. Those who went to Loch Lomond were fearful that the Knebworth gig wouldn't match up, because apart from its awesome vibe, the Scottish setting – at the foot of blue hills and by the banks of a loch – seemed too beautiful to be true. But Knebworth is in a league of its own and, as John Squire joins Oasis for the encores of 'Champagne Supernova' and 'I Am The Walrus', there's a pang of sadness as everyone realises that it's almost lights-up time. As in Loch Lomond and the previous night at Knebworth, the lights-up come in the shape of shimmering, simmering pyrotechnics – thousands of pounds' worth of fireworks.

It's the perfect way to conclude such an occasion. It echoes what's going on in everyone's hearts and also confirms the festive atmosphere that has prevailed throughout. This feels like it has been the biggest party in world – 125,000 of us at a giant, communal sing-song, and now we're going home.

We each of us know we will never witness another night like this. How can Oasis repeat this occasion, let alone better it? 'It's been brilliant to do it but I wouldn't fancy doing it again,' Noel admits. 'We'd love to go back to smaller gigs, but then a small gig for us is now something like Earls Court.'

If, at the time, you'd described the two Earls Court shows, in November 1995, to Oasis as small, they'd have looked at you as if donkey's ears had suddenly sprung from your scalp. By removing an extra bank of seats, each show was able to accommodate 20,000 people, a record in itself. As the band fooled about with a football in Earls Court's vast expanses during the soundcheck, no one wanted to dwell on the prospect of how the hall would look in a few hours' time, packed to the rafters with exuberant fans.

That they were now in the grown-up league was apparent just a few months later when the band announced a show at Manchester City's ground at Maine Road in spring 1996, a taster of what was to come later that summer. As fervent City fans, for Liam and Noel this event would mean a return to the most significant venue of their youth.

For Oasis, their success has happened at the speed of light, too fast and too incredible for them to take in. What's the story? Well, there's the tabloid one that takes the tiniest grain of truth and turns it into an epic fable of mammoth proportions. There's the reality, lost in a fast-moving haze but captured in part by Jill Furmanovsky's photographs. And somewhere in between, there's the rest of us. We too have our memories, bound up in Noel Gallagher's anthems.

Marcus Russell, manager: Maine Road was more like a pilgrimage to their spiritual home than a gig.

Noel Gallagher: I was trying to take it all in, watching everybody go, and it was a weird thing because the lights were all on and it was dark outside. It looked like a big front-room, except there were 42,000 people in it. Maine Road was where we all used to go as kids. So I was standing there, trying to make sure I never forgot this moment. And now I can't remember a fucking thing about it, and yet I stood there for an hour and a half . . . When I look at this picture, I don't hear the crowds roar or find myself standing back on that stage. All I remember is the nightmare of trying to walk out onstage and get to the front of it without tripping over the cables and making a cunt of myself!

Knebworth 08/96

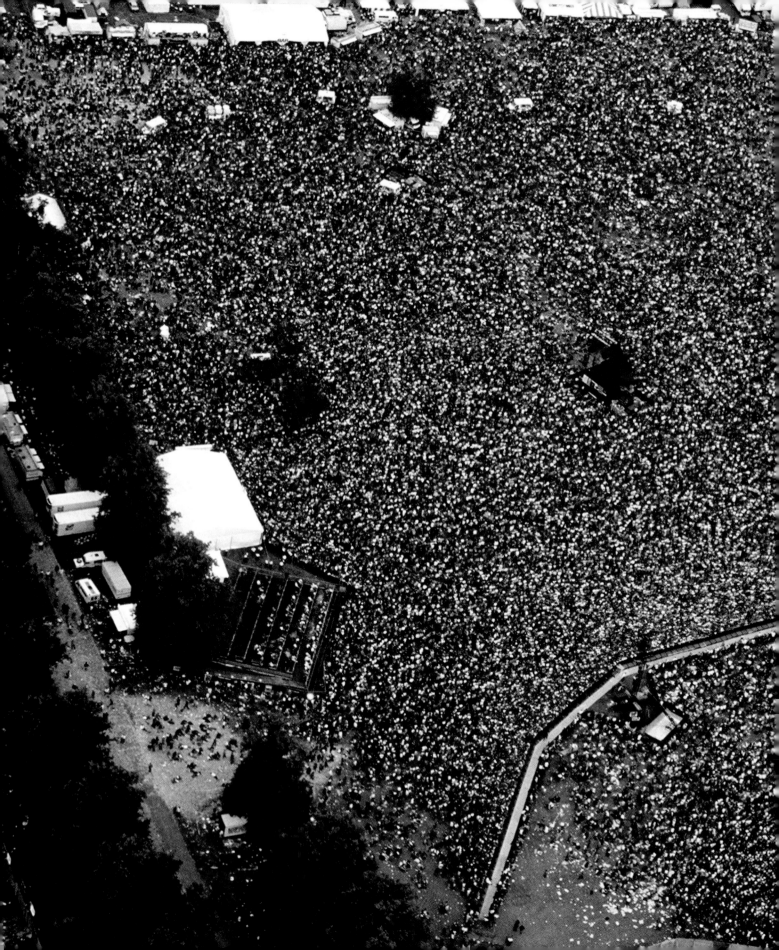

EPILOGUE

June 3, 1997. In her calm Primrose Hill studio, Jill Furmanovsky is showing Noel Gallagher the images she has selected for this book and for her major photographic exhibition, also entitled *Was There Then*, that will coincide with the release of *Be Here Now*. The exhibition will first tour the UK and then, in the course of the next two years, the world.

Noel Gallagher has always shown an interest in which pictures are released of his band. Whenever a new session comes out of the dark-room, he arrives at the studio to cast his eye over it. Today, as he leafs through hundreds of prints, certain images spark his memory or make him laugh. Others make him frown.

It's the first time that he has seen the sum total of Furmanovsky's travels with the band. It's an impressive sight. Her body of work bears witness to their highs and lows, and, if every picture tells a story, the extraordinary rise of Oasis is laid out here for him to see.

It's also interesting to observe the easy relationship that exists between photographer and musician. In the short time that they have worked together, they have each developed a sixth sense of what the other wants.

JILL FURMANOVSKY: *What do you look for when you're going through my pictures making selections?*

NOEL GALLAGHER: I just look for the ones where I don't look a cunt – and fuck everyone else. Just images where everyone looks all right, that Liam looks all right, because he's the one people look at.

I think he's starting to have more of a creative part in the visuals now. He's got his own feeling of what the band should look like.

Well, everybody has, but you can't have five people looking over photographs because it would take for ever. I've been doing it for ages now and I think I can pick a good photograph, even if I say so myself.

What I like about your choice is you tend to pick photographs that are a little bit off the edge.

It depends where they're going. If it's a magazine like *Q* or *Select*, it's a bit more important than if it's a press shot.

Do you like photo sessions, or are they a chore?

They're a pain in the arse. No – it depends who the photographer is. After about twenty minutes, Liam gets bored and he starts annoying everyone, and once he does that it just descends into chaos.

I've recruited him in an unofficial capacity to keep things moving because if it weren't for him doing his antics, you four would just be standing there, wouldn't you?

It depends how drunk he is. I never understood why a photo shoot for the *NME* took three hours. I think it was all a conspiracy, you see, just to keep us out of the pub. The management and the *NME* were in it together. When we started doing photo sessions with you it took twenty minutes and then we could go to the pub and get drunk. So it was like, fuck that, can't we just have Jill doing the photographs from now on?

I know I work quickly . . .

Well, there's no point pissing about is there? If I'm going to spend twenty minutes writing a song I'm damned if I'm going to waste three hours having my photograph taken. There's my comment on that. And if I'm going to take two weeks to record an album, what's three hours of that? Something like 4 per cent – I'm fucking not having that. I think that people take so long shooting photographs because they're unsure of their own ability. When you've got gigs and you give photographers in the pit a photo-pass that allows them to take pictures for the first three songs only, they all start moaning. If you can't take a picture of the singer and the band in the first three numbers there's something wrong with you.

But to defend that point particularly, the thing is that during the first three numbers everyone's getting going. The last *three numbers is when the photographers should be doing it.*

Not with us – we're the same all the way through. Any three would do.

You've said you find being photographed a chore. Do you think you are good at being photographed?

When you do your first photo-session you don't even look at the camera because you're a bit nervous. The more practice you get, the more you get used to having cameras around, the more relaxed you become. Having said that, if there was somebody else hanging round in our rehearsals, I don't think they'd get shots like yours. We'd be a bit too wary of who they were and where the photographs were going to end up.

So control of the photographs afterwards is an important factor?

Yeah. We don't mind if you take a photograph of us really pissed or picking our noses because we trust you to to edit it out, but if it's gone off in a taxi with someone you're never going to see again you think, fucking hell, where's that going to end up?

If you had more control presumably you'd then allow more people in?

You don't want loads and loads of photographs of you knocking around, do you? And I feel that if the photographs are all in the same style it gives the band a certain style as well.

Yeah, one which is basically documentary, that's how I look at it. Even in the studio, not that I've done much there, it's still documentary because it only lasts about fifteen minutes. Occasionally, however – and it is only

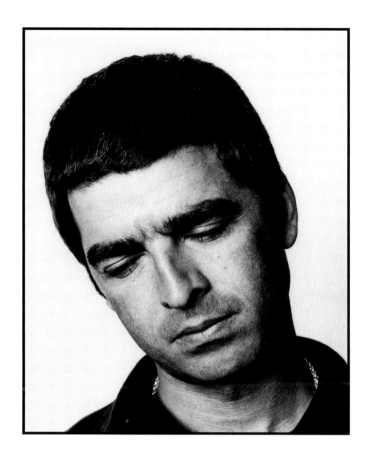

occasionally – you haven't liked stuff I've done. Like the NEC rehearsals in Birmingham where Liam was leaping up and down in the background, you really took against those. Do you remember why?

I thought he looked like an idiot.

But these days he's honed that down to a better way of using that.

Well, he was pissed anyway, do you know what I mean?

If a session produces for you bad memories for example, because Liam's been a pain —

That one in Paris. He was doing my head in – just because it was outside. I don't like having my photograph taken but if you know it's going to be over in twenty minutes it's OK. With Liam, if in between each photograph he's going to go off chasing fucking French people on bikes or pinching their arses, then I become annoyed, because I don't want to stand there for an hour. I don't want to stand there for twenty minutes in the first place, but I *will* stand there for twenty minutes as long as it's only twenty minutes. He knows when he's annoying me; he does it even more until he gets a crack on the fucking head.

Yet that session, interestingly, you let go out, with its mood and all.

I only let it go out because he had a stupid hat on and looked like a cunt

and I looked all right. He looked like a French onion seller, so it was his own fault.

But as you well know, without that insanity that he brings, everything would be so terribly dull visually, and no doubt musically as well—

I don't know about musically, I beg to differ on that one.

Let's talk about MTV Unplugged.

When we went backstage, after having done the show, an MTV official came back and said they didn't get a good take of 'Hello'. So we had to go out and do another one. And Liam decided he wanted to sing it.

I said, well, don't you think it's going to look a bit silly if you only sing one song and for the next hour it's us lot? Of course, he didn't think it was silly at all. It was the most natural thing in the world.

The only thing is, and this is why sometimes I think Liam is a bit psychic really, that the whole Unplugged thing was completely wrong anyway. That set, all those people running around the place, it was wrong, so he sabotaged it for all the wrong reasons.

But we wanted to do it. You don't agree to do something like that and then go out for two days on the piss and not be able to sing, and then slag it off. You either do it or you don't. If you're going to do something you might as well do it. You can't just do half. Do it full-on or not at all.

My feeling these days is that there is now a professional respect between you two.

Mmmm, there always has been as long as he didn't piss me off.

There is no particular band image as far as I can see. There is certainly nothing that's planned – or is there? Maybe it's more subtle and I haven't spotted it.

No, there's not: it's just us being us, really. If you put Liam and Noel standing beside one another it becomes a nineties cultural iconic image, doesn't it? It's only me and our kid, that's how we see it, and our friends see it as Liam and Noel, but to everybody else it's like the faces of the nineties, so I suppose everyone has their own way of looking at it.

When the other members of the band, including Liam, were asked to comment on key points from the past, Liam said 'It's all a blur,' Bonehead said 'Just make it up,' and my feeling was perhaps it's impossible to have a perspective because you're all still in it.

You can never write an epitaph until the story's over, can you?

It did occur to me that because this is a living thing and because you've never stopped—

It's only a short period of time, two or three years.

Well it's not like you've stopped and had six months off to do nothing. When you've had time off you've been writing and doing something else. I must admit that I'm surprised you're still together. When we first met I didn't think the band would last. Do you think that what has happened to you, the success and the fact you can now do as you like, has healed you in a way?

It gives you something to do. If I woke up today, even with all the things that have gone on in the past and all the success and being round the world and having fucking skips full of money, if I didn't have something to do today I'd still be a miserable cunt. Money wouldn't make me, or any one of us really, happy – we all have to be doing something. It's what lies ahead that brings me happiness, as opposed to what's gone on in the past. What's gone on in the past makes you secure, makes you content, because you don't have to worry about shit like not being able to pay the rent any more, but the best thing for me is what's going to happen in the next five years. I don't care what's going to happen in the next five years as long as something happens. Boredom is my greatest fear.

You didn't stay on at school, you didn't go to university, you didn't do any of that stuff – do you ever feel there's some other area you might like to study or go into, or do you feel you've got to take this as far as it can go?

I'm quite happy doing what I'm doing. If I ever have to stop doing this I'll think about what to do next when the time comes.

What price is fame? Privacy, for instance – you've lost it.

To a certain extent, yes, but then again I've just walked down from my house to here and nobody has stopped me in the street. It depends what day of the week and what time of day it is. If you go out to a club on a Saturday night you're asking for it.

Did you weigh it up?

I suppose I thought I was going to be famous but I didn't think it would be this famous. I thought I'd be Johnny Marr-type famous: known to other musicians but not to the tabloids. We soon put a fucking stop to that, didn't we?

I think people are fascinated by you and Liam.

Yep. It's Mick and Keef, isn't it, except Mick doesn't write anything.

You mean that Liam doesn't write anything?

Yeah.

You're going to have to tour this new album for about a year.

Well, you never know. It could be one gig, it could be a year.

Have you thought about that before?

You just try and enjoy each gig because it could be the last one. People always say, well that's really dramatic, but it's fucking true. Liam's voice could go, he could piss me off and I could go: a lot of things could happen. But it would be fun anyway, it would be exciting. ■

Jill Furmanovsky would
like to thank the following
for their support of the
WAS THERE THEN
Photographic Exhibition:

EPSON

HMV